Legacy o

Brian's high school graduation picture from St. Charles Prep High School, Columbus, Ohio, 1998.

LEGACY OF MERCY

A True Story of Murder and a Mother's Forgiveness

Gretchen R. Crowe

Our Sunday Visitor
Huntington, Indiana

27 26 25 24 23 22 1 2 3 4 5 6 7 8 9

Our Sunday Visitor Publishing Division
Our Sunday Visitor, Inc., 200 Noll Plaza, Huntington, IN 46750;
www.osv.com.

1-800-348-2440
ISBN: 978-1-68192-699-5 (Inventory No. T2574)
1. RELIGION—Christian Living—Inspirational.
2. RELIGION—Christian Living—Personal Memoirs.
3. RELIGION—Christianity—Catholic.

eISBN: 978-1-68192-700-8
LCCN: 2022944890

Cover design and Interior design: Amanda Falk
Cover art: AdobeStock
Interior art: Photos courtesy of Rachel Muha

PRINTED IN THE UNITED STATES OF AMERICA

For Brian

And with love and gratitude to our Blessed Mother

Contents

Foreword

Fr. Dave Pivonka, TOR

The phone call that came so early that morning. The Franciscan University student sounded upset as she explained that Brian and Aaron were missing. The police thought they had been kidnapped.

What followed was a tragic week that ended with the terrible discovery that the two young men had been murdered.

As a priest, I'm often asked to explain why such horrible things happen. But what can you say to a mother who has just lost her son? Will anything take away the pain, ease the suffering? What explanation could ever make sense of evil?

I've come to understand that it's not my job to explain the unexplainable nor is it my job to defend God. I don't know why tragedies happen. I do know God is with us, no matter what, and he can do remarkable things, miraculous things, in the midst of the most horrific situations. Good Friday reveals this most perfectly.

Recalling Brian's and Aaron's deaths still brings back difficult memories. Yet, that week of unspeakable sorrow was also one of life-changing grace.

I remember the Franciscan community coming together every evening to pray while the search for Brian and Aaron went on. Sad, frightened, angry young people would fill Christ the King Chapel. They would pray a Rosary, do Eucharistic adoration, and worship with a depth to their prayer that was so authentic and real.

The psalms speak of crying out to the Lord, and our young students were doing just that, crying out to God on behalf of Brian and Aaron and their loved ones. It was difficult to see their pain yet so moving to hear them praying and singing songs of worship.

Amid the darkness, Rachel Muha stood as a shining light. Going through what must be the worst nightmare any parent could go through, she continued to pray and inspire others. I remember Rachel pleading on the local news for those who knew Brian's whereabouts to please tell her. "A mother should be able to hold her son," she said. I could only imagine Michelangelo's *Pieta*, with Mary holding her son close to her heart.

I remember speaking with Rachel once during that awful week. She had a strength about her that moved me. I can't explain it, but she didn't seem to be broken. I am sure she was; no doubt her heart had shattered. But she seemed to have control in the midst of events so outside her control. A faith that knew, even in the unbelievable pain, God was still God. She inspired me then but even more later.

I was in the student union when I first heard Rachel had forgiven Brian's killers. The news swept like a wind through campus. "Have you heard? She forgave them." It was the message of the

Gospel being lived out for all the campus, all the world, to see.

> "Father, forgive them, they know not what they do." (Luke 23:34)

> "Not seven times but seventy-seven times." (Matthew 18:22)

> "If you do not forgive others, neither will your Father forgive your transgressions." (Matthew 6:15)

It was remarkable. Having witnessed this, how could I ever not forgive? On any given day, experiencing miniscule offenses, depending on our mood, we can withhold forgiveness. But not Rachel. She took Jesus' words seriously and forgave what some thought unforgivable.

But that was not the only palpable grace of that week. In addition to students, people came to the campus from all around the area to pray. Christ's Body had once again been broken, and at the same time, healed. God was with us in those moments, and for some present, it left an indelible impression.

Years later, I talked to a priest who lived on campus during that time. Father Conrad had spent his entire career in academia. He was one of the finest Franciscan scholars in the world.

"I remember walking into Christ the King one night," he recounted:

> And the students were worshiping. One of the songs had the words, "I'm forever grateful for the cross." I was stunned. These kids had lost their friends, and they were praying in gratitude for the cross. I began to weep. I had never thanked God for the cross. I had written about it, studied it, and preached about it, but I had nev-

> er been grateful. I was changed that day. My priesthood changed. My faith became more alive, more personal, more real.

Tears formed in Father Conrad's eyes as he spoke. I was touched that years after the darkest week on the campus of Franciscan University, an elderly priest wept remembering how he encountered God in that darkness.

In the end, I suppose this is what I took away. Even in the middle of pain and suffering, God moves on his people, walks among them, and remarkable things happen. Lives are changed, grace becomes real, and God's kingdom comes. I will forever be moved by the beautiful witness to faith by our students, friars, and especially Rachel, whose unwavering witness continues through this book to bring good out of the evil of her son's murder.

Fr. Dave Pivonka, TOR, president of Franciscan University of Steubenville since 2019, worked as the director of conferences on campus at the time of Brian Muha and Aaron Land's murders.

Author's Note

Much of the material in this book came from interviews conducted by the author at various times throughout 2019, 2020, and 2021. Uncited quotes come from interviews with Ken Anderson, Wayne Anderson, Laura Barrera, Bishop Robert Brennan, Debbie Callihan, Nancy Drought, Charles "Travon" Easley, Doug Ganim II, Rick Ganim, Barbara Groner, Daniel Houston, Fr. Mick Kelly, DeShay Mills, Chris Muha, Rachel Muha, Dave and Linda Ramsey, Cassie Seymore, Chad Wilson, and Andrew and Jaime Winkel. I am deeply grateful for their willingness to speak with me.

Introduction

The remarkable thing about the story of the death of Brian Muha and the response of his mother, Rachel, is that once you hear it, you cannot help but become involved in some way. Several people told me this as I was writing this book, and I was no different.

I hadn't heard of Rachel and Brian until colleagues at OSV shared with me that they were looking for a writer to help tell their story. After watching just one interview of Rachel about her work and the motivations behind it, I knew that I had to support her and her ministry in whatever way I could — in particular, by writing this book. That's the effect her testimony and her actions have had on people for the past two decades, an effect that continues today.

I did not regret my decision. In my two decades of working in Catholic media, I have been blessed with the opportunity to tell many good stories of people choosing to do the right things for the right reasons — that is, stories of people who have chosen to follow the path of Christ. In speaking with Rachel, and in getting to know her story intimately, I feel I've been given an opportunity to witness what it means to live the Gospel fully, in the way that the Lord desires for each of us. Rachel's life is not her own; it is a life lived for God and for neighbor. This should be nothing special; it's the life to which each Christian is called. Yet how often do we respond willingly and freely to the One who beckons us? Not often enough. If we did, stories like Rachel's would cease to be extraordinary.

Rachel's story spoke to me in another, more personal, way. Born ten months after Brian, I graduated from high school in the spring of 1999, the same time he finished his first year of college. But while I went on to marry, have children, and have a fulfilling career, Brian's life just … ended. I have spent much time reflecting on the wife who would never meet her husband, on the children who would never be born to Brian, on the patients who would never be healed by him, on the friends who laugh less, and on the family whose hearts will never completely heal. Contemplating Brian's sudden and untimely death has been a reminder to me that we "know neither the day nor the hour" (Mt 25:13). We must always be striving for heaven.

While the May 31, 1999, Steubenville murders affected many people in numerous spheres, this book is meant to be Rachel Muha's story: her story of raising and losing her son; her story of forgiving his murderers; and her story of responding to her son's death not with vengeance or self-pity, but by showing love for others in need. This narrative is not meant to diminish the experiences and involvement of others intimately connected with the events and aftermath of the murders; rather, its purpose is to focus on one specific piece of the overall saga.

The emotions of this story remain raw despite the passage of time. Nearly everyone I interviewed for this book was overcome with emotion at some point during our conversation. I am so grateful to the many individuals who were willing to face the pain of their own loss and experiences in order to speak with me. I am especially grateful to Rachel and her remaining son, Chris, for opening their hearts to me so that I could attempt to tell their story.

Finally, while *Legacy of Mercy* tells the story of an earthly mother whose son was murdered, the compassion of another bereaved mother weaves through its pages. As Rachel walked her most difficult journey with God and not at odds with him, Mary, the Mother of God and the mother of each of us, walked next to her. Mary knew what Rachel was going through, as she knows all of our pain, loss, loneliness, and desperation. She intimately understood the wonder and joy of having a child so full of life, just as she understood the pain of losing him much too soon, and for unfathomable reasons.

It was to Mary that Rachel turned when she was a young mother, inexperienced and overwhelmed with the responsibility of caring not just for the tiny bodies but for the eternal souls of her sons. It was to Jesus through Mary that Brian consecrated his life two months before he died, and both Brian's consecration and death took place on Marian feast days. Rachel is certain, too, that Mary was present at the foot of Brian's cross on the day he died, accompanying him and loving him, just as she had done for her own son.

For these reasons, this book is dedicated, in part, to the Blessed Virgin Mary, queen of heaven and earth but a mother before all else. May her example of maternal devotion, tenderness and care for others, even bravery and determination — qualities that Rachel Muha embodies every day — bring us ever closer to her Son.

Part I

1
The Call Received and the Call that Never Came

When Elizabeth heard Mary's greeting, the infant leaped in her womb, and Elizabeth, filled with the holy Spirit, cried out in a loud voice and said, "Most blessed are you among women, and blessed is the fruit of your womb. And how does this happen to me, that the mother of my Lord should come to me? For at the moment the sound of your greeting reached my ears, the infant in my womb leaped for joy. Blessed are you who believed that what was spoken to you by the Lord would be fulfilled."

— *Luke 1:41–45*

At 2:15 p.m. on Monday, May 31, 1999, Rachel Muha entered what she called "hell as an active state." This was when she received the call informing her that the younger of her two sons, eighteen-year-old Brian, had disappeared.

It was Memorial Day, and in the Catholic Church, to which Rachel and her family belong, it was also the feast of the Visitation — a time when the Church celebrates the Virgin Mary's journey to stay with her cousin Elizabeth while both women were pregnant. The Visitation is a moment where mother greets mother, and the two rejoice in the lives of their sons growing within them. It's a moment when St. John the Baptist, in the womb of Elizabeth, leaps for joy at the presence of the fruit of Mary's womb: Jesus, the Son of God.

Rachel had participated in the Church's celebration at Mass that morning, but by this spring afternoon, there was no longer any rejoicing in the Muha family, only the deepest anxiety and dread.

Brian, along with his roommate and friend Aaron Land, had been taken by force by two other young men on a journey of about twenty miles, spanning three states, that ended in torture and death. It was violence for the sake of violence, spurred on by drugs, anger, barbarism, greed, envy, and a fundamental poverty of love. The events of that day would change an untold number of lives, spanning generations, geography, class, and race.

Jesus, in the Gospel According to Saint John, says, "Amen, amen, I say to you, unless a grain of wheat falls to the ground and dies, it remains just a grain of wheat; but if it dies, it produces much fruit" (12:24). Such was the case for Brian Muha, whose tragic death, while a source of unthinkable devastation and great sorrow, would also bear fruit in the form of life-changing lessons in faith, hope, love, and what it means to forgive.

But none of this was known yet, for Rachel had only just gotten the call. When the phone rang that afternoon, she was sitting at the kitchen table of her Westerville, Ohio, home, chatting with her older son, Chris. On the other end of the line was Steubenville, Ohio, police detective John Lelless. It was a phone call, Rachel would recall later, that "stops you in your tracks, takes you to your knees, clears your mind of everything except this one goal: How to erase the words, 'Your son Brian is missing.' How to erase those words by finding him."

• • •

In the early part of May 1999, Brian Muha finished his first year at Franciscan University of Steubenville in Ohio. He spent the couple of weeks between the end of spring semester and the start of summer classes at home in Westerville, a northern suburb of Columbus (about a two-and-a-half-hour drive west from Steubenville), enjoying some downtime with his mother, his brother, and his hometown friends.

Because Brian was studying to be a doctor — he had a soft spot for children and his eye on a career in pediatrics — his downtime didn't last for long. A summer session at Franciscan would allow him to cross two more courses off his long and demanding list of pre-med requirements. So he packed up again on Sunday, May 30, and headed back to school, planning to stay with some friends off campus in the city of Steubenville for the five-week summer session. Rachel, who had been so happy to have her son home after his first year away, was particularly sad to see him go. Before leaving for eastern Ohio, Brian, in a characteristically thoughtful gesture, arranged to have flowers delivered to his mother the morning after his departure. He would be back by the Fourth of July, he assured her.

Located on the Ohio River near the Pennsylvania border, Steubenville was originally a port town that saw its population peak in the 1940s. The collapse of the steel industry in subsequent decades caused Steubenville's economy to grow sluggish, leading to continuous population shrinkage, widespread poverty, and high crime rates. Having also endured a period of political corruption, the city was experiencing a general decline by 1999. Founded in 1946 by the Franciscan Friars of the Third Order Regular as the College of Steubenville, Franciscan University of Steubenville states that its "mission as a Franciscan and Catholic university that embraces the call to dynamic orthodoxy is to educate, to evangelize, and to send forth joyful disciples." Today Franciscan has an undergraduate enrollment of approximately 2,500 students, the majority of whom are white.

The young men were staying in an off-campus house in the La Belle neighborhood, just southwest of the private university. The neighborhood is — as the *Philadelphia Inquirer* later paraphrased Stephen M. Stern, prosecuting attorney for Jefferson County, Ohio — a place where "different worlds come together." It is not uncommon to see students, men and women religious, and people of different socioeconomic classes coming and going on La Belle's streets. Despite its name, the neighborhood is so well known for being neglected by the city that in 2016, officials pledged to set a plan in motion to address the area's piles of garbage and dilapidated houses.

On a corner in that neighborhood stands 165 McDowell Avenue, an older two-story house into which two young Black men the same age as Brian entered illegally just after five o'clock in the morning on that Monday, May 31. Aaron and a third roommate, Andrew Doran, were in bedrooms, and Brian was sleeping on the couch in the living room.

The two perpetrators wanted Rachel's Chevrolet Blazer, which Brian had parked outside the house. They repeatedly hit Brian and Aaron in the head with a gun. Blood splattered everywhere.

In the other bedroom, Andrew woke up and, hearing sounds

of violence, exited through a window to go to a nearby house to call the police. But first he opened a side door and called to his friends to see if they were OK. Before he ran for help, Andrew heard one of the assailants say, "Oh [expletive], we got another one."

Once the intruders knew they had been seen, what had begun as a violent robbery turned into a violent kidnapping and a gruesome double homicide. Brian and Aaron were forced into the backseat of the Chevy Blazer and driven east on Route 22 toward Pittsburgh. In Washington County, Pennsylvania, the two perpetrators stopped on the side of the road, marched their two captives up a hill into a wooded area, shot both in the head with a .44-caliber handgun, and left them for dead under a wild white rose bush. The entire series of crimes had taken less than forty-five minutes, but it would be four and a half days before the bodies of Brian and Aaron were found.

• • •

Two hundred miles away and several hours later that Monday, Rachel was deeply anxious. Brian was missing, and blood had been found in the house where he had been staying, the detective had told her over the phone. Rachel had to suppress every maternal instinct and desire to drive immediately to Steubenville to help look for him. Instead, as this was before the widespread use of cell phones, she was instructed by the police to stay home in case Brian called.

"You know how slow time goes when you are waiting for someone to call?" Rachel recalled later. "Every second was like a slow torture. I repeated over and over again in my mind, a thousand times, 'Brian, call me. Brian, call me. Brian, where are you? Brian, call me.' The call never came." Chris sat with her, a combination of "misery and leadership," Rachel said. "He was suffering, and yet he wanted to protect me."

Rachel and Chris called everyone they could think of who knew Brian and Aaron. No one knew where they were. They called family, including Rachel's sister, Debbie Callihan, who was tasked with informing the rest of their large family. Many family members, including Rachel's younger brother, Rick Ganim, and his wife, Diane, mobilized to make the journey to Rachel's home in Westerville. "As we pulled in the driveway, there were candles lit in the window," Rick, who is Brian's godfather, recalled.

Flying in from Florida, Rachel's parents, Richard and Betty Ganim, were picked up at the airport by close family friends Dave and Linda Ramsey. "When they walked in, I witnessed the saddest moment," Debbie recalled in a diary she kept during that time. "Our parents were not able to help us. Isn't that what parents are supposed to do? Make things better for their children. Watching my parents hold their daughter who was sobbing and them sobbing, not being able to do anything else was the worst. I will never forget the look in my dad's eyes as he just stood and held her for the longest time."

Rachel also called Fr. Vincent Michael Scanlan, TOR, president of Franciscan University, to tell him that Brian and Aaron were missing. He said he knew. "Father, they won't let me come to Steubenville to search," Rachel told him. "I have to stay home in the hopes Brian will call here. Father, I can't come and look for my son." Father Scanlan responded: "Rachel, he is our son, too. All of the friars here are his spiritual fathers. We will go out and look for him."

"Picture that beautiful scene, that beautiful act of love," Rachel wrote later in a letter to family and friends. "Friars, in their long robes and rosaries, walking door to door and asking everyone if they knew anything about the two missing Franciscan University students, Brian and Aaron." Not only did the friars search, but they prayed. They celebrated Mass for Brian and Aaron and held prayer vigils in the university chapel every day that week.

Back in Westerville, a small vigil was taking place at Rachel's home. Those gathered had learned from police that the Chevy Blazer had been found that evening in Steubenville with two men in it, and that one had escaped. There was no sign of Brian or Aaron.

"At that point, it was: Sit tight," Rick said. "And so we just sat there. There was nothing we could do. We didn't know the severity of it yet, except we knew that it was bad." Debbie wrote, "We prayed and prayed. Every time the phone rang we jumped, but nothing. Finally, at midnight, we went to bed."

Of course the phone never did ring — at least not with the call for which everyone was so desperately praying, the call with news of Brian's safe recovery or with Brian himself on the line. Every moment of the waiting was agony, and Rachel could do nothing but rely entirely on God to get her through it.

The next morning, Tuesday, while Rachel continued to wait by the phone, Chris and Rick decided to drive to Steubenville. They made flyers and hung them around campus and the surrounding neighborhood. "There wasn't any game plan. None of us had obviously experienced this before," Rick said. "You just figure it out as you go. At that point, you're trying to fix it. You don't know what else to do."

First thing on Wednesday morning, with the permission of police, Rachel also left for Steubenville. She recalled: "I didn't ask any questions. But I'm thinking, 'Why all of a sudden can we come now?'" The horrific truth bubbled up from a place deep inside of her that she didn't want to acknowledge: "They think Brian can't call home anymore."

Unwilling to think the worst, Rachel told herself that Brian was just too far away from a phone to call. She was anxious to join the search, though the thought was daunting. "I tried to picture Steubenville and all of a sudden a small town became a huge expanse of land, buildings, hills, waterways — a seemingly impossible task to find two missing boys," Rachel later wrote privately. Still, she was glad to be on her way.

Rachel headed east, riding in silence with her friends the Ramseys and her sister Debbie. She left Brian's parting gift of flowers — received on Monday morning just a few hours after his violent death and a few hours before she received the call from the Steubenville police — on a table in their home. Beside the pink vase filled with white roses was a card in Brian's handwriting that had arrived with the flowers: "Just wanted to say hi, even though I am away. Love, Bri."

2
The Muha/Ganim Family

Beloved, if God so loved us, we also must love one another. No one has ever seen God. Yet, if we love one another, God remains in us, and his love is brought to perfection in us. This is how we know that we remain in him and he in us, that he has given us of his Spirit.

— *1 John 4:11–13*

Experiences of trauma bind people together. This is one of the few comforts of having to confront something as horrendous and incomprehensible as violent, senseless death — especially of the young. Brian Muha's death had such an impact on a group of his peers from Columbus. This group of a dozen or so young men who attended high school with Brian are emotionally bound for life out of love for their classmate and brother whom they lost when they were all still too young.

This group is bonded in a concrete way, too: through identical bronze arm tattoos of the initials *BCM*. For these men, the tattoos, acquired in the year following Brian's death, are a permanent and visible reminder of the friend they all admired and an unspoken commitment to emulating him. For most of them, it is their only tattoo. That is the mark that Brian Muha made on the lives of the people who knew him. Because before Brian died, he lived.

• • •

Brian Charles Richard Muha was the second son of Charles (Charlie) and Rachel Muha. Born on July 23, 1980, in Cleveland — the birth city of his older brother, mother, father, and maternal grandfather, Richard Ganim — he was a lifelong resident of Ohio. His maternal grandmother, Betty Ganim, was born in Washington, DC, but spent the majority of her life in Cleveland.

All of Rachel's grandparents had immigrated to the United States from Lebanon and Syria in the early 1900s. Rachel's mother's family was Syrian Orthodox. Her father's family was Maronite Catholic, an Eastern Catholic rite in full communion with Rome, and they were heavily involved in the Maronite community in Cleveland. Their church, which Rachel's grandparents helped to build and where she received the Sacraments of Baptism, Confirmation, Eucharist, and Matrimony, was named after Saint Maron, the founder of the Maronites.

Born in Syria in the middle of the fourth century, Saint Maron was a priest who later became a hermit. Renowned for his holiness and for working miracles, including healings, he inspired a following that, after his death in 410, became the Maronite Church. In 405, St. John Chrysostom, an early Father of the Catholic Church known for his preaching and public speaking, wrote to Saint Maron asking for his prayers and expressing his love and admiration, saying, "We keep you in our memory continuously, carrying you around in our soul, wherever we are." Over the centuries, many miracles have been attributed to his intercession.

In early-twentieth-century Cleveland, immigrant families, including the Ganims, were poor, and they struggled, but they were also determined to contribute to the life of faith in their community. Saint Maron, the church they built together, started out in a small, rented house. Eventually, the community was able to come together to build a formal church on Carnegie Avenue, and there it remains. Both of Rachel's children were baptized there.

Growing up, Rachel was surrounded by a large family (she was one of five children — four girls and a boy) and an omnipresent faith, the importance of which was passed down from generation to generation. "My father's parents — they eloped because my grandmother's parents didn't want her to marry my grandfather," Rachel said:

> And so they literally eloped and came to the United States totally on their own. Those stories are told over and over: of their determination, their love for each other, their strength, their poverty, and their commitment to God, who got them through everything. And even though they lived in a very small house with their fourteen children as they were growing up, they wanted to build that church. They wanted to have that beautiful place of worship.

Rachel, a petite woman with dark hair and a warm smile, grew up attending Catholic school, surrounded by her close and loving family. "We're second generation, but we're 100 percent Lebanese. And Lebanese people are very family oriented, very religious — and that is us," Rachel's brother, Rick Ganim, said. When Rachel's father, Richard, was in his mid-thirties, he attended a Cursillo retreat and came home on fire for his Faith. Shortly thereafter, her mother, Betty, had a similarly moving experience. The parents witnessed the faith and love of Jesus to their children, of whom Rachel was the second oldest.

In high school, Rachel met Charlie Muha, also from a big family with a strong Catholic foundation, though his roots were Hungarian and Irish rather than Lebanese. They were married in 1973, when both were twenty, and Rachel took some college courses and worked in a few office jobs. Though Rachel and Charlie eventually divorced — their marriage was annulled in 1992 — they first welcomed two sons into the world. On December 13, 1978, when his parents were twenty-five years old, Christopher was born. Brian followed nineteen months later on July 23, 1980. Ten months after that, the young family moved from Cleveland to a home in Westerville, a suburb of Columbus. That home became the only one Brian would ever know.

• • •

When the Muhas first arrived in Westerville, a new neighbor came over to welcome them, and before she even said hello to Rachel, she bent down and directly addressed the two dark-haired boys at their mother's side. "She gave them total attention, and I was so grateful to her. She noticed my sons, and she's treating them like human beings," Rachel recalled. "I thought, 'I have to remember that children are real human beings.'" It was a lesson that she took to heart and always remembered.

Rachel wanted to be extremely intentional about raising her boys in the Catholic Church, deliberate about passing on the faith she had received from her family. She wanted her sons to know, above all, about God's infinite love for them. With no Maronite church nearby, the Muhas became members of St. Paul Catholic Church in Westerville, one of the largest parishes in the Diocese of Columbus. Rachel registered the boys right away for the parish school, joining a long waiting list. At Mass every Sunday, they sat in the front pew so the boys could see and better pay attention. "Every time at the consecration, I would whisper to the boys, 'Here comes the miracle,'" Rachel remembered. "She had a special way about her, being a mom," recalled Linda Ramsey, a close family friend who met Rachel through Columbus Right to Life.

The boys grew up playing in their Westerville neighborhood, riding bikes and spending time with friends. Brian liked to pretend to be Superman, wearing his red and blue Superman shirt everywhere. Over it, though — like every superhero concerned about his secret identity — he wore a white button-down shirt and a little sport coat. "For a while," Rachel recalled, "I had Clark Kent with me everywhere: at Chris's soccer games, at the grocery store." When someone was in trouble, however, the sport coat and white shirt came off, and it was "Superman to the rescue!"

When Rachel needed to earn some money to help offset expenses, she started babysitting for kids the same age as Chris and Brian, and as a result, the boys had built-in playmates. She also helped with clothing drives and bringing food to the needy — including one family at St. Paul that had fifteen children. "I think helping with the clothing drives and all that made me realize how lucky we are, how blessed we are, and how there's people who need help and we should help them," she said. "I think that planted a seed."

Chris and Brian attended St. Paul Elementary School, where they served together at daily and Sunday Mass, and at weddings and funerals. When the boys were nine and ten, Rachel and a few friends began a weekly "play and pray" day on Fridays for their kids and their friends. The kids would have a snack, play at the park, learn about a saint, and pray some prayers. And then they'd play some more.

"At first it was ten kids for a couple months," Chris recalled. "She just started small with the people she knew and it just kind of organically grew from there. As people heard about it, they came and experienced it." It grew to seventy to a hundred kids playing football or basketball, or on the park equipment at one of the local parks in Westerville. The gatherings were so successful that some of the parents, including Rachel, decided to band together and start a school, which they named *Christifideles*. They found a building a ways out from Columbus that, at its peak, hosted about seventy students.

The year that Rachel began the play group, she and the boys went on a group pilgrimage to Medjugorje, the small village in Bosnia-Herzegovina that is believed by many to be the site of Marian apparitions, though the apparitions are not officially approved by the Catholic Church. For the first few days, Brian was sick to his stomach, but he refused to stay behind at the boarding house. "It was hot, the days were long, and we were walking a lot," Rachel remembered. "Brian came along every day, and in between stomach problems, he spent his time smiling at and giving little presents to the children of the village."

Rachel recalled how Brian and his friend Michael wanted to climb Cross Mountain — the highest mountain in the vicinity, atop which sits a large concrete cross with a relic of the True Cross of Jesus — barefoot as an offering for Michael's older sister, who had just been diagnosed with a brain tumor. "The hill has sharp rocks, and the boys were only nine, so I said they can climb the hill but not barefoot," Rachel wrote later in a private letter:

> The boys objected. I told them that God knew their desire and he knew that I said no, so they will get graces for Michael's sister because of their desire and their obedience. Brian gave me a look — the kind of look that said, "You got me but I don't like it one bit." Still, he didn't say anything. Dejected-looking, but with their shoes on, those two nine-year-olds climbed the hill, prayed at the top, and came back down.

When they arrived home from Medjugorje, the Muhas learned that the brain tumor had been successfully removed. Michael's sister went on to marry and have children.

Rachel found other ways to get involved with the faith community. She was active in Greater Columbus Right to Life and Ohio Right to Life, working to protect the unborn. The pro-life movement was a cause to which she could lend her voice, and she was able to work on behalf of it at home, modeling a love for life through her actions and priorities, while the boys were sleeping. Through this ministry, she became friends with Fr. Kevin Lutz.* The family took to him, and so Rachel decided to attend Mass more frequently at Holy Family Church in Columbus's inner city, where Father Lutz was the pastor. She hoped that change would help reengage her boys, who, nearing their teenage years, had started getting restless at Mass. She also hoped that joining a parish in an underprivileged part of town would further foster her sons' compassion for others.

It seems to have worked. As Brian grew into a young man, he frequently volunteered at a local hospital. He also tutored

---

*In 2019, Fr. Kevin Lutz was credibly accused of sexually abusing a minor and was removed from ministry. His name has been added to the Diocese of Columbus's official list of credibly accused priests. The diocesan website states, "For purposes of this list, a credible allegation is one which, based upon a review of the available facts and circumstances, is more likely than not to be true." "List of Credibly Accused Clergy," Columbus Catholic, Diocese of Columbus, https://columbuscatholic.org/chancery/list-of-credibly-accused-clergy.

children at a community center — a foreshadowing of his later desire to work with children and of his mother's future. When Brian was thirteen, he traveled to Denver for World Youth Day, a global celebration of faith for young Catholics, and saw Pope John Paul II.

As a child, Brian suffered from a weak back and was unable to play sports. During his middle school years, he also suffered from migraines and had problems with his heels. He knew what it was like to endure pain for seemingly no reason, and it taught him perseverance. By the time he got to high school, his health problems resolved themselves, and he played every sport he could.

In 1998, Brian graduated from St. Charles Preparatory School in Columbus, an all-boys school where he was an honor student involved in student government and a standout athlete. That fall, he began attending Franciscan University, where Chris was going to be a sophomore. Knowing he wanted to become a doctor, Brian began taking courses that would help fulfill that dream. Outside of class, he played and coached flag football and organized a group to drive to the March for Life in Washington, DC, in January. He also made time for a little mischief: He and some friends rearranged the furniture in the common room of their dormitory — and got written up by the school for their antics.

While the boys were at Franciscan, Rachel got to know some of their university friends, including Chris's Christian fraternity brother Mick Kelly, who remembers her as unique among the other parents he knew. Even before the tragedy, "We all knew that there was something different about Rachel," recalled Mick, now Father Mick, a priest of the Diocese of Arlington, Virginia, ordained in 2010.

"I don't think that we would completely have been able to articulate the profound admiration we had for her — and the sense that this is a good woman," he said. "She would go to Mass. She would pray her rosary. She would speak devoutly. She was never overpious. She was just this really genuine, gentle, peaceful woman."

It was on Franciscan's campus that so many of Brian's friends and family members would gather during that heart-wrenching week to organize their search for him, praying and hoping that this beloved son, grandson, brother, nephew, and friend would be returned to them.

It was not to be. But the terrible search, in God's great providence, was to bring about something even greater.

3

The Search and the Decision to Forgive

If one has a grievance against another; as the Lord has forgiven you, so must you also do.

— Colossians 3:13

"Rachel, you know what God wants you to do, don't you?"

Rachel Muha was standing in a remote field in rural Ohio, a borrowed cell phone pressed to her ear. Her son Chris moved about nearby, looking, calling out his brother's name. On the other end of the line, hundreds of miles away in New Jersey, was Martha Favreau, one of Rachel's close friends. The two women had taught religious education together, raised their kids together. Now they faced every parent's worst nightmare together: a child missing. A child feared dead.

"You know what God wants you to do."

It was early afternoon on Thursday, June 3 — the second day of the community's search for Brian Muha and Aaron Land, but the fourth day since the pair had gone missing. It would still be one more day before the bodies of the boys were found on that roadside hill in Pennsylvania. Before the finding came the searching, the waiting, the hoping, the dreading, the praying.

• • •

Every morning of the search for the two boys began at Franciscan University with Mass; each evening ended with a holy hour. Among those searching were Brian's brother, Chris, and their uncle, Rick. From the moment they had arrived in Steubenville on Tuesday, the day after Brian and Aaron went missing, the two had been hanging flyers and looking. They talked to people, scouted around abandoned houses — did anything they could think of to find a clue that might tell them where Brian and Aaron were. Brian's father, Charlie, was also present, having flown in from Texas on Monday to take part in the search.

On Tuesday night, more than a hundred students, faculty, and staff attended a holy hour of prayer in front of the exposed Blessed Sacrament — whom Catholics know to be Jesus Christ himself — in which they recited fifteen decades of the Rosary, praying for the students' safe return. Chad Wilson, a friend of both Brian and Aaron, who was on campus for summer classes when they were abducted, recalled how those gathered prayed, searched, and kept hope alive while waiting for news about the young men.

On Wednesday, when Rachel arrived in Steubenville, she was totally focused, totally prepared. She had maps of the city and a job to do. She organized the family groups of searchers and told them where to go. "There was so much area to cover," Rachel's sister Debbie recalled. "Were they in the town, were they in the river, were they in the woods? We just had no clue. We searched the neighborhoods, under porches, in dumpsters, abandoned houses, anywhere." Debbie remembered observing the police taking cues from the vultures and wondering what they were doing — until she remembered how vultures feed. "So wherever they were, we kind of went," she said.

"The plan was to do everything we could to look for them," recalled Chris Muha. "We weren't being told where they had been. We had the sense from the police that they weren't alive, but we genuinely believed [there was] a chance they were still alive. We didn't know any details about anything, so we were just looking everywhere."

"I'll never forget taking my arms and putting my hands together so that [Rachel] could step on my hands and climb into the dumpster," Linda Ramsey remembered years later, "because she thought maybe they had thrown him in there."

Another of Rachel's sisters, Betsy Marnecheck, drove to Steubenville from the Cleveland area with her five-month-old daughter, Faith, to help with the search. Betsy pushed Faith in the stroller up and down the streets of Steubenville, asking people if they had any information about where Brian and Aaron might be.

The search, reported on by local and national media, was a days-long slog that involved members of local and state law enforcement from Ohio, West Virginia, and Pennsylvania (the three states on the portion of Route 22 traversed by the perpetrators), and even the FBI. The Associated Press reported how "police and 100 volunteers including troopers on horseback picked through briar patches, waist-high grass and swamps for three days." In Cleveland's *Plain Dealer*, Mike Pirraglia, chief of the Colliers, West

Virginia, volunteer fire department, described the conditions and attitudes he observed: "Real tough terrain. There's a lot of briar bushes that are making it hard to search. You can't give up hope. You've got to keep at it. You've got to keep plugging."

The public search, however, was just one part of the developing case. While family, friends, community members, and volunteers scoured the city, another search — the official investigation — was being led by Detectives John Lelless and Charles Sloane of the Steubenville Police Department. By Wednesday morning, their search had yielded two suspects in custody — two young men who most definitely knew more than they were saying. From the suspects, police were gleaning clues mired in conflicting stories and blame. They were beginning to piece together a grisly puzzle that involved not only the abduction of Brian and Aaron, but also another assault and another stolen automobile in Pittsburgh. As law enforcement began to get more information from the suspects about where they had been on the day of the killings, the law enforcement–led search expanded from Ohio along Route 22 into West Virginia and Pennsylvania. Police let the families know that they had suspects in custody but shared little other information.

By Wednesday, the public search had expanded to include members of both boys' families, including more than forty members of Rachel's family who had traveled to Steubenville from the Cleveland area and from Florida, as well as friends and volunteers. And on Thursday, the Steubenville police chief called a meeting at the police station. There, he told the families that police suspected "foul play."

"I had no idea what that phrase meant, so I thought, 'Well, this was useless,'" Rachel recalled. It wasn't until much later that she realized what the police had been trying to tell her. "It means they suspect death. … And I look back at that, and I think, 'Why didn't he just say it, you know?' Maybe it's too hard to say it to a mother — to two mothers."

The searchers continued their mission, but with a limited scope, per the police. Later, Rachel would discover that the police had intentionally sent the families to a place where they knew they wouldn't find what they were looking for. "Now I can look back and say that they thought they were doing the right thing. They didn't want us to come across Bri," she said. But while hindsight offers clarity of vision and understanding, Rachel felt during those terrible days that she and the other searchers were being unnecessarily prevented from doing what they needed to do — what Brian needed them to do.

It was a horrible week, filled with panic and fear, recalled Fr. Mick Kelly, who was then a student at Franciscan. "You don't expect badness at Steubenville because you're generally wrapped in an atmosphere of loving goodness," he said. "You don't expect evil to break out like that."

Rachel had no choice other than to rely completely on God throughout the whole terrible time:

> We were totally dependent on him to get through every single second because I couldn't get through every second by myself. It was the worst, longest, most painful ordeal ever, and it wasn't a pain because I was in pain. It was a pain because I knew Bri was either in pain or had suffered pain. And that's totally different. I couldn't care less what I was feeling. I was so heartbroken that Brian was somewhere hurting. He had been hurt. He had been beaten up or he had been shot, but then he was alive somewhere and I couldn't get to him. I didn't know where he was. He was suffering and he was wondering — you know, in my mind, he's wondering — "Where are they? When are they going to come and help me?" And I couldn't get to him.

Despite the great suffering, the goodness and kindness of people was seemingly unending. As Rachel's sister, Patty Muha, and her husband, Jamie (Charlie Muha's brother), were driving up from Florida with their young kids to help with the search, they were stopped for speeding. When they explained why they were rushing, the policeman's response was: "You stay safe. I will clear you all the way to Ohio." A ways down the road, the family's car got a flat tire. When the mechanics found out that they were related to one of the missing boys, they cleared the service bays, fixed the tire immediately, and got them back on the road. "It just went on and on," Debbie recalled. "Every time we turned around somebody else was doing something."

The local Super 8 gave the searchers every room, did their laundry, and provided them with food. "It was an amazing engulfing of our family," Debbie said. "We would go into a restaurant to eat, and there would be no bill." Someone else showed up with ten cell phones — still a rarity in 1999 — that helped them stay in touch with one another as they searched different parts of town. "I can never say enough about how [well] we were treated," Debbie recalled.

By Thursday, things looked grim. The two men in custody continued to blame one another and send the police on wild goose chases. So much was unknown, and Brian and Aaron still had not been found. Rachel was devastated. She told the Columbus Dispatch that day: "My heart is filled with sorrow. I have to have Brian back. My arms are aching to hold him again. I hope Brian is just hurt somewhere and he needs us."

• • •

"Rachel, you know what God wants you to do," came Martha's voice.

On that desolate Thursday, standing in that field with her

ear pressed to a donated cell phone, Rachel understood what her next step needed to be. When her friend's call had come in, Rachel had been praying the Lord's Prayer — the prayer that Jesus himself taught his disciples to pray — over and over in her head as she searched for Brian: "Forgive us our trespasses as we forgive those who trespass against us." What did those words even mean? What does it mean to forgive? So much more, she thought, than she had ever understood before.

"I know," Rachel replied. But she was torn. Her mind raced as she prayed for clarity. What is this that you want me to do, Lord? What does it mean? Does it mean I'm supposed to say the people who hurt my son shouldn't be punished? Does it mean I'm supposed to say that what they did is OK? That they had a good reason? Is there any good reason ever for doing something horrible?

That night, at the prayer gathering inside Christ the King Chapel on the Franciscan campus, she gave voice to her decision. Standing in front of a group of 250 family members, friends, students, volunteers, and reporters, Rachel Muha said out loud the four words that would change everything: "I forgive these men."

Her words floored everyone except her son Chris, with whom she'd talked it through. "I don't think any of us could believe what we were hearing," Debbie said. Brian and Aaron hadn't even been found, and Rachel was publicly forgiving the men who had most likely killed them. "That was the turning point for everybody," Debbie said. "You just can't not take her lead." Linda Ramsey recalled, "We all sobbed, and I was thinking, 'How can she do that?' God was with her, and she was more or less trying to guide us in the right direction."

Rachel's profession of forgiveness changed the tone of the search, Rick recalled, adding that he believes her statement warded off potential feelings of hatred or hardening of hearts that might have been creeping into Brian's family and friends at that terrible time. "To be able to believe it, not just say it, was, I would say, life-changing to everybody there," he said. Father Kelly said, "It's hard to understand how heroic that is; it's hard to see how heroic it is to forgive until someone is really put to the test."

While sin has a ripple effect, so does love. Rachel's decision to forgive that night — an act she has chosen again and again throughout the years since Brian's death — changed her life and the lives of many others. In the moment, her words calmed the anger, frustration, doubt, and hurt of family and friends. With reporters present in the chapel, her comments made the newspapers and extended outward beyond the Steubenville community. The *Plain Dealer* reported that "Muha's mother, Rachael [*sic*], talked of the pain of her loss but said she forgave those who were responsible."

The Prodigal Sons, a group affiliated with Franciscan University and to which Aaron Land belonged, were profoundly affected by Rachel's profession of forgiveness. One of them, Ivan Ortize, was interviewed by the *Pittsburgh Post-Gazette*: "[Her declaration of forgiveness] has helped me," Ortize said. "Right now it is very easy to hate and to condemn all of society. She has helped me with my reaction. 'What would Jesus do?' is a real catch phrase today. But what she did is what he would have done."

Rachel's words set the tone. She met hatred, including wishing the perpetrators harm, with a hard no. Justice and punishment are necessary, yes. But so is forgiveness. "Rachel was saying: 'I don't want to let them off the hook. That's not what I'm trying to do with forgiveness. I want what's best for them. And part of what's best for them is to pay in this life for the crimes against my son, now, rather than to pay for it in the next life,'" Father Kelly recalled. "That's so much more loving than letting people off the hook." Debbie remembered, "Her strength was an inspiration to all of us. So many people told me that throughout this ordeal, they were most touched by her steadfast beliefs."

Why did she do it? "God is good," Rachel said, simply.

After her decision to forgive, Rachel felt peace — the peace that the Lord promises when one actively chooses to follow where he is leading. "Somehow, I knew it wasn't a peace telling me that Brian was alive," she recalled. "But it was a peace like I've never felt before. It was a calmness. It was an acceptance of what was going to happen — of what did happen, and what was going to happen." Being at peace, however, did not mean that the hurt went away. "It was a painful peace, because I wanted Brian back," Rachel said.

That wish was never to come true. The next day, less than twenty-four hours after Rachel's declaration of forgiveness, the bodies of Brian and Aaron were found under the bush bearing white roses, wild kin of the flowers delivered to her just hours after their deaths. Rachel believed them to be a sign, observed the homilist at Brian's funeral Mass, "from another Mother who lost a Son long ago."

Even as Rachel publicly forgave the two men who had likely beaten and murdered her son, she knew that she would have to renew that act of forgiveness frequently in coming months. As time passed, she would rely greatly on those around her who loved her, including Rick, who cut out all the photos accompanying newspaper articles about the case and upcoming trials so that Rachel could read them without seeing the suspects' faces.

Why? "I didn't want to hate them," she said.

4
Nathan and Terrell

Bear one another's burdens, and so you will fulfill the law of Christ.

— Galatians 6:2

Two men are physically responsible for the deaths of Brian Muha and Aaron Land. Their names are Terrell Rhaim Yarbrough of Pittsburgh and Nathan Da Shawn (known commonly as "Boo") Herring of Steubenville. Both were eighteen at the time of the murders, and both are still in prison for kidnapping and killing Brian and Aaron. Their crimes were shocking and devastating, and the law saw to it that justice was served.

But while Terrell and Nathan carried out the beating, abduction, and murder of the two students in May 1999, they are far from the only ones culpable. To understand this, one must know their stories — where they came from, and how they came to be. And to know their stories is to know the stories of thousands who have come before them and who are on the streets now — and thousands who, unless something drastically changes, will follow similar paths.

• • •

In the aftermath of the murders of Brian and Aaron, rumors swirled — rumors that emerged from attempts to understand why the tragedy had happened. Why them? Why death? Why that way? Some said that the two students had been abusing drugs; some said that they had known Terrell or Nathan or had interacted with them before that fateful day in May.

Those rumors were false.

Terrell and Nathan had never seen, spoken to, or interacted with Brian or Aaron until the early morning of May 31, when they broke into Brian and Aaron's apartment. After beating the boys with a pistol, Terrell and Nathan grabbed the keys to the Chevrolet Blazer parked outside — the prize they had come for — and forced Brian and Aaron into the Blazer's backseat, bound for Pittsburgh and that hilltop off of Route 22.

While autopsies later proved that there were no drugs or alcohol in the systems of either Brian or Aaron, the same was not true for Nathan and Terrell, who habitually abused both. On the day leading up to the murders, Nathan had smoked pot, drunk beer, snorted cocaine, and popped pills. By that point in Nathan's life, John Angelotta testified for the defense in his trial a year later, that behavior was chronic. "In the year before the crime, he was an all-day user," Angelotta, a clinical counselor specializing in substance abuse, said. "His life pivoted around pot, alcohol, and cocaine. I don't think he saw a relevant sober moment throughout the entire year." Terrell was also a chronic drug user with a history of violent behavior.

So it was in a drug-induced, mind-altering haze that Terrell and Nathan marched their two victims up a hill in Washington County, Pennsylvania, and shot them in the head on that Memorial Day morning. Taking Brian's credit and ATM cards and some cash, they left the bodies there, walked back to the car, and drove on to Pittsburgh. There, around 6:30 a.m., they were caught on camera unsuccessfully trying to extract cash from an ATM machine.

Later that afternoon, the two perpetrators drove to Squirrel Hill, a Pittsburgh neighborhood, to steal another car. According to trial testimony, they targeted Barbara Vey, owner of a green BMW. Attacking her on a stairwell landing in her apartment building, Terrell and Nathan demanded the keys to the car, and Nathan threatened to kill Barbara. Terrell stood between the two. After Barbara had retrieved the keys from her apartment, Terrell told her, "I saw you earlier and I wanted you to be my girlfriend." Then he kissed her. The men left, Nathan behind the wheel of the BMW and Terrell driving the Chevy Blazer, and Barbara called the police. She later said that preventing one kiss wasn't worth her life.

On the drive back to Steubenville that evening, the Blazer ran out of gas, and Terrell was assisted by a passing motorist by the name of Brian Porter. When he got back to town, Terrell met up with a friend, Brandon Young, who was only sixteen at the time. That evening, they drove together around the city in the Blazer and were spotted by police. The two left the car and ran down the street. After a chase, police caught Terrell and arrested him on charges of receiving stolen property (the Blazer). Later that night, around 8:00 p.m., police also found Barbara's BMW. Brandon surrendered to police on Wednesday morning.

Once in custody, Terrell lied about his name and any involvement in the day's crimes. He denied knowledge of Brian and Aaron and denied that he had anything to do with the stolen Blazer. Around his neck, though, he wore an incriminating and devastating piece of evidence: Brian's rosary, which police removed. He deflected attention from himself by giving authorities Nathan's name.

Police did not have Nathan in custody until Wednesday morning, June 2, when they picked him up on his way into court for an unrelated matter. Under questioning, Nathan blamed Terrell for having shot and killed Brian and Aaron. That afternoon, Terrell again spoke to police; confronted with Nathan's testimony, he now admitted that he had been involved in stealing the Chevy and abducting the two boys. But he was adamant that it was Nathan and Brandon who had shot and killed the students. Terrell directed police to look along Route 22 for the bodies, and on Wednesday afternoon, Ohio authorities asked Pennsylvania State Police to join the search. Later that night, when police searched a crack house where Nathan had been living, they found Brian's credit and ATM cards.

As police were piecing together evidence (now with help from the Federal Bureau of Investigation), Terrell talked again on Thursday, June 3, this time agreeing to show police where the bodies had been left. He took them to the place along Route 22 in Washington County where a few days earlier he and Nathan had forced Brian and Aaron out of the Blazer. It was getting dark, so police postponed their search of the area until the next day. Eventually, late Friday afternoon, after a full day of searching, a team of nonfamily searchers found the remains of the two students lying in heavy vegetation near the spot Terrell had indicated.

• • •

It would be very easy to discard Nathan and Terrell as evil, or as the worst of society, and to leave it at that. They were eighteen, legally adults. But a closer look at their lives gives a deeper understanding of how they ended up as they were, and where deeper faults might lie.

Court proceedings indicated that Nathan, a Steubenville local, hadn't always been a bad kid. Once upon a time, he had been a good student, even captain of his middle school basketball team. He'd had good manners and made decent grades in school. He hoped his athletic ability could help lead to bigger and better things. But the odds were stacked against him. His parents were both addicted to drugs and spent time in prison, so he was left to raise himself. In eighth grade, Nathan also broke his leg, hindering his promising athletic ability.

The real turning point, however, came a couple of years before the injury, when Nathan's older brother, Derrick, drowned in a lake in Mississippi while trying to cool off from the heat. The family had been traveling to Louisiana, where Nathan, a track star at age twelve, had been invited to participate in the Junior Olympics. Devastated, Nathan blamed himself for his older brother's death and gave up the sport.

After a while, according to court testimony, he dropped out of school and became addicted to drugs and alcohol like his parents. His dad attempted "tough love" to get him back on track, but it backfired: His son left the house and never returned. Nathan met Terrell and liked his big talk — but most of all he liked that Terrell would say, "I love you, dude." Nathan said at the trial, "I never had anyone express their feelings to me, and it felt good." So, according to Nathan's trial testimony, when Terrell came to him saying he knew where they could do a robbery — what he called an easy "in and out" — Nathan went with him.

For his part, Terrell grew up in Pittsburgh but later moved by himself about forty miles west to Steubenville's inner city. As a child, he had been neglected, unsupervised, and — worse — shuttled among family homes depending on who was in need of the welfare check. His father, who was dying of AIDS that he'd contracted via intravenous drug use, would call his son "Money" or "Dollar" because having Terrell around meant receiving a welfare check. His mother was a heroin addict who was in and out of prison for theft. Terrell was described at his trial in 2000 as "a feral child on the streets who had never been to the dentist and quit high school in eleventh grade."

Neglect, indifference, drugs, alcohol, death — this is how these boys grew up. They were stricken with a poverty of love, and Terrell and Nathan are far from the only people culpable for who they became.

"All those adults around — they're the ones that should have been in prison too," Rachel Muha said years later, recalling the testimony at the trials that painted the picture of Terrell and Nathan's childhoods:

> Those are crimes against humanity, crimes against a child. But the child ends up paying, because he grows up, and he's angry, and he's lonely, and he's unloved. And he lashes out. And more times than not, they lash out at a stranger because the really difficult thing to understand is [that] even the people who have harmed them, in their minds, deserve their love.

And the cycle continues. At the time of his trial, Nathan had a girlfriend who was pregnant with a baby boy.

• • •

It wasn't until the trials, held more than a year after Brian's death, that Rachel learned about the lives of Terrell and Nathan. "I thought, my goodness, these two boys — and who knows how many more — didn't stand a chance," she said. "What a waste of two lives. Who knows what they could have done."

While driving to the courthouse for Nathan and Terrell's trials — the courthouse for Jefferson County, Ohio, is located in inner-city Steubenville, where Nathan grew up and where Terrell and Nathan met — Rachel began noticing the children standing at a bus stop in the mornings. "I would look at the children and think, 'Maybe Terrell and/or Nathan stood at that very bus stop — maybe they stood there,'" she said. "And I realized they weren't born killers. They became killers."

As Rachel listened to Terrell and Nathan's stories, her mind began to swirl with ideas of what could and should be done. "There're children growing up like that everywhere," she recalled thinking. "There're children growing up like that in Columbus, Ohio, and I've been to Holy Family Church in the inner city. I've seen it, and what am I doing about it? And what would Brian do about it?"

These were questions that would remain at the forefront of her mind throughout the trials, and they were questions that would change the course of her life.

5
Chris and Brian

Let love be sincere; hate what is evil, hold on to what is good; love one another with mutual affection; anticipate one another in showing honor.

— *Romans 12:9–10*

A critical part of this story, which cannot be underscored enough, is that the perpetrators and victims were peers by the measure of age — but peers raised in two very different sets of circumstances. Terrell Yarbrough and Nathan Herring were eighteen years old and products of inner-city life, surrounded by a culture of substance abuse and parental neglect. Brian Muha was eighteen years old, the cherished son of Rachel and Charlie. Aaron Land was twenty years old, beloved by his mother, Kathleen O'Hara, and by his late father, Howard M. Land, who had died seven years before. Brandon Young, for his part, was only sixteen. None was old enough even to legally share a beer with the other.

There was another boy in the mix, too — another victim whose young life was forever changed by the events of May 31, 1999. Chris Muha was only twenty years old when his younger brother was beaten, abducted, and murdered. He and his parents were left to pick up the pieces following Brian's death — to find a way to make sense of the senseless and to cope with the enormous loss.

Chris's life, in many ways, was from then on defined by what was no longer there. A vacancy, a gaping hole, replaced his maturing relationship with the little brother with whom he had ridden bikes, played ball, and driven to and from high school and college.

• • •

The first memory Chris has of Brian is playing at the end of the street in Westerville, near the home where they grew up. Brian, all of two or three years old, ran up to Chris, grabbed his arm, and bit him. "I just remember running home crying," Chris recalled, with a laugh.

But the memory has lingered in retrospect because of what it conveyed of Brian's personality — even at such a young age. "Looking back later in life, [you can see that] Brian had a fire to him," Chris said. "You can see how that developed into a part of his personality." Brian, Chris added, would always stand up for people. "He always had a fierceness and a determination and loyalty about him."

Only Terrell and Nathan know the details about what happened when they entered 165 McDowell Street in Steubenville on that Monday morning. The police officers who arrived on the scene found the place empty, with furniture knocked over and blood in the living room and on Aaron's bedding and in his room. But Chris can make a few informed guesses about what went on. "I have no doubt that whatever happened in the house, that Brian would have been — it never would have crossed his mind to run," Chris said. "His instinct always would have been to help Aaron. I have no doubt that throughout all of it he would have stood by Aaron and done whatever he could to help."

Growing up, the two Muha boys rarely argued and never fought physically. And though they were only nineteen months apart, Brian looked up to his big brother. Chris related a story of the brothers running outside with their little white dog, Silver, when Chris was around six or seven years old. Chris was running or riding a bike, and Brian was trying desperately to catch up with him but just couldn't. "Brian got really sad and either fell down, or he just was sad that I wouldn't slow down for him, and ran home crying," Chris said. "I remember that staying with me, and later it kind of hit me how much he looked up to me and wanted to be like me."

At play or while serving Mass, the boys did much together, but they also had different interests. Brian loved the thrill of BMX dirt bike racing, and Chris took up football and basketball. They both loved playing video games; some of Chris's favorite memories of their childhood were made when they were in the basement taking turns at the console. "I just remember being down there for long stretches of time playing these long quest-type games with him and trying to figure out how to get to the end until Mom would tell us to go outside or come on and do homework or whatever," Chris said.

It was finally at St. Charles Preparatory School, which they attended only a grade apart, that the siblings began to become close friends as well as brothers. Brian joined the football team, where Chris was already a standout running back, spending his first year on the freshman team. But his speed and skill earned him a spot on varsity the next year, with Chris as the other starting running back.

Andrew Winkel, a friend from St. Charles, said that when Brian joined the team, he "came out with a vengeance." After having a physical condition that prevented him from playing sports for the first part of his life, "it was like [he had] fourteen years of pent-up energy that he just wanted to get out," Andrew recalled.

For the next two years, Chris wore number 5 and Brian wore number 6. He was "an incredibly gifted athlete, just naturally," Chris said, and the two played on the field together for many Friday nights. "That was just a lot of fun because everything about what we were doing was the same," Chris said. "We would get ready for each team each week and ride home from the games afterward to talk about what we did right and wrong. Those were some really cool moments."

During Chris's senior year and Brian's junior year, they ran together and were elected by their classmates as student council president and vice president, respectively. It was another example of how their relationship had become more personal, more meaningful, more mature. "He became less of a little brother and more of a brother," Chris said, and they could talk about everything — from their parents' separation a few years earlier, to the big game coming up on Friday night, to girls, to future plans. The big brother/little brother dynamic faded away, and they were peers. "We were both playing on the team together, and we were both thinking about our futures in college, and we [could] sort of talk about what we wanted to do with our lives and about our family," Chris said. "He was the one person who could relate most closely to everything [I was] going through."

At the same time, the boys kept their independent identities. Chris was more overtly religious — his nickname on the football team his sophomore and junior years was "Father Muha" because he wouldn't use swear words and avoided smoking, drinking, and partying. When Brian joined the team, the coach tried to call him "Little Muha," but Brian corrected him. "I'm Brian Muha," he said. Brian became friends with a group of guys who tried some of those more typical high school experiences.

Over time, Chris began to understand what Brian saw in those young men. "I came to appreciate what those guys had in spades, and what Brian had in spades, was an authenticity and a pureness of heart." Brian inspired loyalty in his friends — the same friends who now have his initials tattooed on their arms and many of whom are involved with Rachel's current work. "It's not a fleeting thing for them. It's twenty years later. They're still really intimately involved, and they're all really close still, I think partly because of Brian," Chris said.

During the summer after Chris graduated from high school, he and Brian went on a group pilgrimage to Fátima, Portugal, the site of a series of Marian apparitions to three shepherd children in 1917. The pilgrimage, organized by Rachel, included about twenty-five people, mostly young people Chris and Brian's age, that they had gotten to know through school and church. In Fátima, many pilgrims make a painful but grace-filled "walk on their knees" to the chapel there as an act of reparation for the sins committed by humanity against Christ and against one another. Everyone in the group except one girl wanted to do it, and no amount of talking convinced her. "Too painful, not fun," she said. So instead of making this act of reparation with the group, Brian stayed back with the girl. He spent a lot of time with her on the pilgrimage, and on the last day of the trip, she changed her mind. She and Brian made the walk on their knees, both crying, both happy.

During this trip, Brian was picked to carry the statue of Our Lady of Fátima in a procession. He bought a replica statue to bring home to Rachel, who had not gone on the pilgrimage, carrying it on his lap the entire flight rather than risking its getting damaged in the cargo hold. To this day, the statue has a place of honor in Rachel's home.

Brian's senior year in high school was filled with classes, sports, a trip to American Legion Buckeye Boys State (an educational summer leadership program focused on government), and even a role in a school play called *Wild Oats*, where he had one line that he delivered with gusto. "When the bad guys were caught, [Brian] came in and said, 'Y'all under arrest now!'" Andrew Winkel recalled. "He must have practiced that line for three weeks trying to get it right and absolutely crushed it."

A year after Chris began college at Franciscan University, a couple of hours east of home, Brian followed suit. Brian had been torn about attending the school, wondering if the community would accept him as himself and if this very Catholic university was the right place for him. "He just wasn't overtly religious in the same way that I was or comfortable in that kind of environment the way that I was," Chris said, reflecting on the different ways the two boys lived out their faith.

At the last minute, he decided to give Franciscan a try. The school had offered Brian a scholarship, but Brian — to the slight chagrin of his tuition-paying parents — asked that it instead be given to someone who needed it more. "It was darling when I thought about it because he had that much faith in us that we would agree with him," Rachel said. "That just came totally from him, and I was so proud of him."

During the one year the two brothers shared on campus, Chris still avoided the party scene, while Brian was more comfortable with it. They would occasionally eat lunch together, play intramural flag football, or just hang out together. The brothers coached the football team of one of the women's households on campus. And they drove to and from school together at breaks, time that was reminiscent of those drives to and from high school and home from football games. "We were the only two people sharing those two worlds," Chris said. Brian also began dating.

In the spring semester of 1999, just months before Brian was killed, Chris asked Brian if he wanted to consecrate himself totally to Mary through St. Louis de Montfort's spiritual program. Chris had done it the previous year, as well, and he "wanted to get [Brian] more involved in the practices of the Faith beyond Mass." Brian agreed.

"This was something that I wanted to do together with him to build our relationship and be closer but also give him something that I thought was good," Chris said. For thirty-three days, they got together, either in one of the chapels on campus or in one of their rooms, to read, pray, and prepare their hearts for the consecration. On the solemnity of the Annunciation, March 25, when the Catholic Church commemorates the visit of the archangel Gabriel to Mary of Nazareth, Brian made his total consecration to Jesus through Mary at Franciscan's Christ the King Chapel. On that special feast day, the Church recalls how Gabriel informed Mary that God found favor with her and that she was to become the mother of his Son, Jesus. Mary changed the course of humanity when she humbly responded with her fiat: "Behold, I am the handmaid of the Lord. May it be done to me according to your word" (Lk 1:38).

The chapel where Brian and Chris professed together their desire to love and serve the Lord through his mother, Mary, was the same sacred space where, a little more than two months later, searchers and other members of the community would gather daily to pray for Brian's safe return.

• • •

A few months before Brian died, Chris had felt a desire to pray for Brian in a special way. He didn't know exactly why — maybe because of the temptations of college life or being around girls more. But on that fateful Monday, when Chris read the note his brother had written to their mother to accompany the flowers he ordered for her, he got a strong sense that Brian was going to be away for a long time, and that he now needed to be praying for his brother even more.

As the events of the next few days unfolded, Chris began to understand that intuition. And on the evening of Friday, June 4, 1999, the older brother who had transitioned from playmate, to protector, to adviser, to peer suddenly found himself an only child.

6

The Finding and Its Aftermath

Where, O death, is your victory?
Where, O death, is your sting?

— 1 Corinthians 15:55

The bodies of Brian Muha and Aaron Land were found by a team of searchers on Friday, June 4, at 5:15 p.m., about one and a half miles west of the McDonald exit of Route 22 in Robinson, Pennsylvania. They had been left at the top of a hill about a hundred feet from the eastbound lanes of Route 22, near Candor Road.

Rachel was not with that team. After a day of searching in

the Steubenville area, she, Chris, and a few other people had headed to the local police station for what had become a regular evening briefing for the families. Most of the force was out searching, except for Ken Anderson, a young police officer who worked in the identification division. Rachel stuck her head into Anderson's office and said she was there for the briefing. Anderson told her to head upstairs to the courtroom where the briefings had been taking place, and that someone would be with her shortly. She did as he directed.

Then the phone rang. On the other end of the line was Detective Charlie Sloane, who was working the case with Detective Lelless. "I answered the phone, and all he said was, 'They found them,'" Anderson recalled.

Anderson told Sloane that the family was there for the briefing. Sloane responded that, because of all the cars and emergency vehicles at the scene, he and Lelless couldn't get out. "He said, 'You're going to have to tell her,'" Anderson recalled. "And I said, 'I can't do that.'" Sloane responded that he had to; it was only a matter of time before the media figured out what was happening, and the families needed to hear it from the police first. Anderson agreed, hung up the phone, and stood up. He knew what he had to do, but he had never made this kind of notification before in his six years on the force.

"We'd spent several days with these people, so I knew it would kind of be a relief, but at the same time to have to confirm someone's worst nightmare is not an easy thing," he recalled. Anderson walked slowly up to the courtroom and paused just outside the door. Even twenty years later, he still remembered the scene vividly:

> There was Mrs. Muha, where she always was. She was in the back row, sitting by herself, praying her Rosary, just kind of with her head down. I walked in, and I knelt down,

> and I took her hand, and I said, "They found them." And she jumped up, and she yelled, "And they're alive?" At that moment my heart sank. This woman never gave up hope, even after all those days, that they were still going to be found alive. And I just said, "I'm sorry, they're not."
>
> And this is the part that gets me, and I'll never forget this. I was sick for her. I had just confirmed her worst nightmare. But this woman, she takes me by the hand, she pulls me up, and just gives me the biggest hug. And she squeezed me tight, and she whispered in my ear, "Thank you for everything you've done." At that moment, I'm thinking, "This woman is the most amazing person I've ever met — but also an incredible mother." I think she felt and could tell my sadness, my pain, and she instantly felt the need to comfort me. I've never met anyone like that in my life. To hear those words and the first thing you worry about is somebody else — and that somebody was me — I've never forgotten her.

Rachel then proceeded to tell the rest of her family gathered at the station, exchanging hugs and sharing in mutual sorrow. "The feelings were just too much," Rachel's sister Debbie recalled. "Watching Rachel, Charlie, Chris, and everyone else was more than you can imagine. We were numb. There is no way to describe the feelings of that evening." Rachel's brother, Rick Ganim, said: "To see that is terrible, but to experience it like she did is a million times more terrible," he said.

After three days of intense searching, emotions were as high as the loss was deep. Even the police officers were crying. "Everybody there was a mess. You become their family in three days," Debbie recalled. "We were like family to everybody."

For the first time in five days, Rachel knew the whereabouts of her son, and she wanted to see him. The arms that had rocked

Brian as a baby and guided him through eighteen years of life longed to hold him once more. If that wasn't possible, she at least wanted to rest her eyes upon his face.

• • •

It was not to be. The boys' bodies had been exposed to the elements for more than four days, and Rachel was told over and over again that viewing her son in such a state would be excruciating. Dental records had to be used to tell the bodies apart. Though it broke her heart, Rachel acquiesced. She never saw Brian again.

There were people who did see Brian, though — the police, the coroner, and others at the scene, including Fr. Michael Scanlan, then president of Franciscan University, who traveled to the remote Pennsylvania hilltop to bless the bodies. Rachel never forgot that kindness. When Father Scanlan died at the age of eighty-five in 2017, she wrote in a memorial tribute:

> He climbed the hill that Brian and Aaron climbed and he knelt by their dear bodies — and he prayed. He prayed. He raised his voice, hands and eyes to heaven and prayed for his sons. When Father came back to campus we were waiting for him. His face had changed. He looked so much older. Sad. Almost even traumatized. He had seen man's inhumanity to man.

As word of the discovery spread on campus Friday night, reporters interviewed university students and staff as they wrestled with the reality of what had happened.

"We are stunned. We are sickened," Carole Brown, the director of evangelistic outreach on the campus, told the *Pittsburgh Post-Gazette* at the time. "We pray for repentance of those who committed the crime and forgiveness by those of us left to pick up the pieces."

Fr. Mick Kelly — the priest of the Diocese of Arlington who was then a student at Franciscan — was interviewed as he went into the chapel, fighting back tears. "I don't think it's necessary to ask questions [about why the students were killed] right now," he told a reporter. "It's necessary to mourn the loss, to come together as a community of Christians who can offer the family support and pray for them. No one will ever have a satisfactory answer. It's not always good to ask why. It's important to see what we can do to help."

Years later, Father Kelly recalled the magnitude of what Rachel had to face — and how she faced it with such Christian fortitude. She showed "bravery in the face of suffering, in the face of being out of control of your world," he said, and did it "with great love for everyone. I've never seen anything like that in the world."

At a prayer service that night, Father Scanlan and the Rev. Calvin McLoyd, then pastor of Second Baptist Church in Steubenville, encouraged the families to turn to God in their suffering. "This situation that has invaded your family — this is not a total reflection of the citizens of Steubenville," Rev. McLoyd, the Black leader of a predominantly Black church community, said. "We have a common bond. We have a common denominator that makes us brothers and sisters in Christ. We share your grief, your sorrow, your loss."

On Saturday, June 5, once the bodies had been removed by Washington County Coroner Timothy Warco, the area searched, and the crime scene sealed, the families were able to visit the site. Rachel climbed the hill that her son had climbed, and she kissed the ground where his blood had been poured out, "making it holy ground," she said in her eulogy at Brian's funeral the following week, "a precious piece of earth."

Debbie Callihan recalled the pilgrimage to the scene of the

crime that took place after lunch on Saturday:

> The road we went on was not much of a road, and the people who lived back there were very kind to let us plow in. We had about ten cars. After a short hike in the woods, we were there. There was the orange paint used to mark the area under the trees where Brian and Aaron were found. Above them were the most beautiful wild white roses. The ground was very moist and dark. We could actually smell the blood. But it was comforting to know where he was found. It was just too much to bear, and Rachel was not doing too well then.

"I saw her go to her knees and put her face right where she thought Brian's blood was," recalled Linda Ramsey, who had been with Rachel every moment of the search. "She picked up a twig. She said, 'It's Brian's blood.'" They prayed, and they were able to smell the roses. "It was almost a sign that Brian was OK," Linda said.

"It was like a field of stars, these beautiful, perfect white blossoms on this hidden part of this highway in Pennsylvania," said Father Kelly, who brought Rachel a branch from the bush. "It was just white and beautiful and a painting out of the Dutch Masters, and then utterly painful to think Brian's blood watered that bush. Like everything that week, it was utterly painful and utterly beautiful all at the same time."

Chris planted the branch in their backyard, where it blooms every May.

• • •

One Catholic tradition holds that Mary is the originator of the Stations of the Cross because she would retrace the steps of her

Son's passion and death after he was killed on Calvary. Rachel believes she understands why: "She wasn't torturing herself," Rachel said. "She was reliving her Son's last moments on earth when he was visible to her, and I totally understand that now."

Even twenty years later, it is especially hard for Rachel to contemplate how Brian was killed.

> When he was found, I thought: "He went through that hell all by himself." He and Aaron had to suffer that horrible ordeal. And he couldn't even call us. He couldn't call out to us. He was so alone. We were two and a half hours away and didn't know what was happening to him. And I hate that. People will say to me, "I'll bet he didn't feel anything. I'll bet that at that moment that that trigger was pulled, God took him." Well, maybe, but probably not. I mean we all have to suffer our Calvaries. But right after that moment, he was free.

She takes great comfort in knowing that even though Brian was physically separated from his loved ones during his final hour, he wasn't alone. "That's the difference between the hell Bri went through and the hell real souls in hell have to go through," she said. "Bri had his guardian angel. He had Jesus. He had the Blessed Mother. He had the cloud of witnesses."

• • •

As Cindi Lash and Ann Rodgers-Melnick of the *Post-Gazette* reported on June 5, 1999, "The discovery of the bodies of two missing Franciscan University students on a remote Washington County hillside crushed the hopes but not the faith of hundreds of their relatives, friends and classmates, who for five days flooded heaven with prayers for their safety and their return."

This faith continued to be on display on Sunday, June 6, when the university held a memorial Mass on campus. It was the first of two services that the school arranged in memory of the two students — the second would be in the fall, when campus was filled again, minus the lives lost over the summer.

The early morning liturgy, celebrated in Franciscan's Christ the King Chapel, was packed, with an overflow crowd forced to worship outside. Rachel and her family sat in one of the front pews. Seventeen priests were present, including Father Scanlan and Father Augustine Donegan, who at the time ministered at Franciscan's campus in Gaming, Austria.

It was Corpus Christi Sunday, a time when the Church draws the attention of believers to the Most Holy Body and Blood of Christ and what it teaches about his True Presence in the Eucharist. The prayer after reception of Holy Communion reminded worshipers of the fleeting nature of life on earth — for Brian and Aaron, yes, but for every other person, too: "Lord Jesus Christ, you give us your Body and Blood in the Eucharist as a sign that even now we share your life. May we come to possess it completely in the kingdom where you live forever and ever."

"No other day in the year is more fitting for a memorial Mass than this day," said Father Donegan, adding that the Eucharist must be the object of our focus, for in the Eucharist we celebrate the promise of eternal life. "Everything [else] is passing away. That is the one thing that is usually forgotten by most people. That which we have today, we will not have tomorrow."

After the Mass, about 150 people processed southwest from the chapel through the streets of Steubenville to 165 McDowell Avenue, where members of Brian's and Aaron's families stood on the porch and received flowers.

As the Steubenville police continued their work, the wheels of justice had begun to turn. On Friday morning, Nathan and Terrell had already appeared in Steubenville Municipal Court, where they were charged with kidnapping, aggravated burglary, and aggravated robbery. They entered no plea. Brandon Young, the sixteen-year-old who had been in the Blazer with Terrell on the night of the murder, was charged with delinquency by means of receiving stolen property.

Judge Richard Powell ordered a preliminary hearing for June 11 and set a $2.2 million bond for each defendant. Rachel would not attend the hearing; crushed, heartbroken, and not wanting to hate the young men, she knew she could not allow herself to see their faces.

Stephen M. Stern, prosecuting attorney for Jefferson County, Ohio, stated his desire for prosecutorial jurisdiction over all of the crimes encompassed in the case — a point that turned out to be critical in the coming years. "This crime began in our community against residents of our community," Stern said at the time. "Citizens of this county should try the perpetrators of this heinous crime." After some back and forth, Pennsylvania ceded jurisdiction, meaning that two murder trials — one for Nathan and another for Terrell — would be held in the city from which Brian and Aaron had been abducted.

But well before the court proceedings began, the family and friends of Brian and Aaron had to bid their final farewells to the young men.

7
Remembering Brian

For if we have been united with him in a death like his, we shall certainly be united with him in a resurrection like his.

— *Romans 6:5 (ESV), printed on Brian's funeral Mass program*

Just south of the Scioto River in Columbus, Ohio, sits Holy Family Catholic Church, built in the German Gothic style. The church has been an integral part of the Franklinton neighborhood of the state capital since 1877, when it was established as the fifth Catholic parish in the city. While it was common at that time in American history for Catholic parishes to serve a particular ethnic community, Holy Family's parish history notes that it was unique in that it was founded to serve all people in the area, regardless of place of origin.

Holy Family Church is a beautiful structure in a less than beautiful part of the city. The neighborhood scouting website Area Vibes gives Franklinton an F crime rating, noting that the neighborhood has a crime rate that is 151 percent higher than the national average, with a violent crime rate of 129 percent higher than the national average. The church, with its imposing brick in the front and its quiet Marian grotto in the back, is a beacon of hope for the neighborhood. It operates Holy Family Soup Kitchen, which serves hot meals to up to two hundred people each weekday. It also provides basic food items, clothing, and hygiene items.

Rachel Muha began to bring her sons to Mass at Holy Family when they were in grade school. And it was in this church that Brian's soul was commended to God during his Mass of Christian Burial on Wednesday, June 9, 1999, at 11:00 a.m. Then-pastor Fr. Kevin Lutz, who had become a friend of the family, presided.

• • •

The night before the funeral Mass at Holy Family, a wake was held from 4:00 p.m. to 9:00 p.m. at Egan-Ryan Funeral Home in Columbus. It was the biggest wake the funeral home had seen in twenty-five years, Rachel's sister Debbie recalled. More than a thousand people came to pay their respects; the line never slowed down, and didn't end until 10:45 p.m. Two prayer cards had been prepared for the funeral — one with the image of Our Lady of Fátima and the three shepherd children, and the second with a representation of Michelangelo's Pietà, in which Mary cradles her dead son, just taken down from the cross, in her arms. The accompanying verse from the fourteenth chapter of John read:

> Let not your heart be troubled: ye believe in God, believe also in me. In my Father's house are many mansions: if it were not so, I would have told you. I go to prepare a place for you. And if I go and prepare a place for you, I will come again, and receive you unto myself; that where I am, there ye may be also. (1–3, King James Version)

On Wednesday, the church was filled beyond capacity with one thousand family members and friends. Mourners filled the choir loft and the side aisles of the church; some stood at the front of the church by the two side altars, dedicated to the Blessed Virgin Mary and Saint Joseph. Members of the media were also present.

But it wasn't the throngs of people that made Brian's funeral memorable, nor was it the thanks given to God for the life of one who died so young in such tragic circumstances. What set Brian's funeral Mass apart was the overt call to conversion at the heart of it. In his homily, Father Lutz said:

> God did not will this tragedy as something that would please him; rather, he has taken this tragedy and has sanctified it, so that it will bear fruit in the lives of thousands. The fruits of prayer, grace, and conversion are already manifested in so many ways.
>
> It is only when things seem totally beyond reason that faith can guide us.

He added:

> Everything about this tragedy lacks reason, but faith tells us that this may be the greatest moment in our lives to know and love God more. A moment of intense evil has been turned into a call to holiness for all of us. The

> precedent for this is Calvary, where the greatest moment of evil, the killing [of] God's only Son, became the call to holiness for all who would look on him whom they had pierced.

Father Lutz reiterated this call to conversion in his final words of reflection on what people could do for the Muhas in their time of trial. The family, he said, doesn't need any more flowers or any casseroles. They are looking for more.

"They feel that the greatest honor and tribute to Brian would be the living of your life for Christ," Father Lutz said:

> Be holy. Love Jesus Christ. Love his bride, the Church. Imitate Mary who contemplated always the things of God and who stood faithfully with her Son even in the darkest hours of Calvary. Receive the Eucharist often. Be swift to forgive. With the knowledge that Brian has eternity, he would only want us to spend each day in our quest for God. If we could only look beyond the veil that separates this life from eternity, we would regret every wasted moment. This is now the moment in which God asks us, in fact he commands us, to be holy.

Indicative of the great emotion of the day, Charlie Muha, Brian's father, said, "My heart is aching," but was unable to continue. In his eulogy, Chris Muha, just twenty years old, reflected on the potential fruits of the shocking event, especially in the country's secularized culture. These fruits included the thousands of people from all over the world who were united with them in prayer — "many perhaps who have not prayed in a long time"; parents finding renewed realization of the gift that their children are; greater exposure to the merits and community at Franciscan University; and the many acts of charity enacted toward the Muha family.

He made a direct appeal to the mourners to turn to Christ — especially amid a suffering so difficult to comprehend:

> The inability to perfectly communicate our suffering is one of the reasons so many despair in their sufferings. We must turn, then, to the One who knows us completely, who has numbered even the hairs on our heads. Only with God can we perfectly communicate our suffering, and thus suffering provides us with a unique opportunity for conversion. Only then is the question "Why?" that distinguishes human suffering sufficiently answered, and only then will we fully realize that Brian's death and our suffering [are] not in vain.
>
> It is now up to each one of us as an individual to make sure that Brian's death was not in vain. We are all here because of some connection we had to Brian, whether it be intimate or indirect. It is not by accident that we knew Brian, and it is not by accident that we are here today. We might think of ourselves as threads on a spider web, brought together by God from many and varied places, with the death of my brother at the center. God has brought you here to speak to you. Do not let the death of my brother be in vain for you. Brian is with God, and wants nothing more than our total and deeper conversion to him.

Rachel's remembrance examined Brian from a multitude of angles, as if looking through a prism: Brian as a friend, a boyfriend, a brother, a cousin, and a son. But the story was the same from all angles: The eighteen-year-old had been a person of love, a person who cared deeply for others and who planned to dedicate his life in service to them. He had been a young man who kissed his mother every morning, every night, and every time he left the house or came home — who said "I love you" every time he said goodbye. In fact, "I love you" were the final words ever exchanged between mother and son — when he called the night before he died to let his mother know he'd made it back to Steubenville safely.

Brian had been a person of love, and Rachel's invitation, offered in the midst of her own brokenness and sorrow, was for everyone to follow in his footsteps by imitating the One who is love himself. "[Brian's] life and death have brought us great blessings," she said, adding later, "Now, Brian is healing souls and mending hearts and binding us in love. Please don't lose the grace of this moment. Cling to love."

The funeral was also another opportunity to encourage forgiveness in the face of evil acts — a theme that would continue in the months and years to follow. "Christ loved, loves, and will love forever; Christ forgave, forgives, and will forgive forever; and we are called to imitate him, especially in the face of the greatest test," Father Lutz said in the homily. "That is where the true disciples are known."

Following the funeral Mass, Brian was buried at Resurrection Cemetery on the north side of town. When the funeral cortege departed from the church for the cemetery, Debbie recalled in her journal, "The line of cars was so long that the police escorts actually closed the ramps and the highway was ours alone."

• • •

Two more memorial Masses honoring Brian took place later that summer: The first was held just for Brian on Sunday, July 18, at St. Maron Church in Cleveland, where he had been baptized. And another celebrating the lives of Brian, Aaron, and two university employees who had died over the summer was held at Franciscan University on Thursday, September 2, after students returned to campus. Approximately one thousand members of the community came together in prayer, and those who had died were honored when roses were brought to the altar during the offertory procession.

Finally, a commemorative cross was placed by the community at the site of the slayings, with a crown of thorns surrounding the crux and rosaries hanging from one of the beams.

After Brian's death, the administration of St. Charles Preparatory School planned to retire his number 6 jersey, but football coach Matt Strausbaugh, who had coached Brian and Chris on so many Friday nights, had a different idea. Instead of retiring Brian's number, he proposed turning it into a living legacy, establishing a tradition that continues to this day. Each freshman football class is told about Brian — about his qualities, his virtues, and his great care and consideration for others. When each class begins its senior year, the players vote for the individual in the class who most emulates Brian, and that young man wears number 6 for his final year. More than twenty young men have worn number 6 in the past two decades. Each player chosen to wear number 6 receives from Rachel a handmade rosary and a card "thanking them for being somebody that Brian would have loved to know," she said.

"I am just so grateful that [the coach] thought of that because Brian lives, you know," said Rachel. "And the young men who wear his number — they're so proud to be chosen to be number 6."

In the days and weeks following Brian's death, other tributes came pouring in — tributes that spoke to the character, virtue, and jovial nature of the young man who was suddenly gone. Growing up, Brian would make his cousins laugh by telling jokes and putting in false teeth, his family remembered. "He was always smiling and always did what other people wanted," said Jackie Muha, a cousin who also proclaimed one of the readings at Brian's funeral Mass.

On an online memorial site set up in memory of Brian, another cousin, Erin Callihan, wrote, "If for only 18 short years we had him here, I will never for one second wish away the pain of losing him for the chance to have never met him."

Brian was called a "model kid," a "dedicated athlete," and someone who would do anything for a friend. But he was also "free-spirited" and was remembered as someone who loved playing pranks. "He always had a glint in his eye. He was fun-loving and mischievous," said Mike Federer, whose son Mike served as a pallbearer. Another St. Charles student, Benjamin Witten, testified to Rachel how her example and words at the funeral had changed him from a "devout agnostic" to a person of faith, and showed him how to lead his life. "I must also thank you for your amazing strength," Benjamin wrote to her that same day. "It was also through your faith that I was able to see God. I admire all of you for the strength you possess and am honored that I have had the opportunity to witness and share in your love and faith."

Years after Brian's death, friends still fondly recalled what Brian had meant to them. Chad Wilson, a St. Charles graduate and fellow Franciscan student who was friends with both Brian and Aaron, recalled how their lives "have had a forever impact" on his own. The great sorrow that he faced, however, has been transformed — instilling in him a passion for life, an attitude of care toward his community, and a desire to help work to break the cycle of violence.

"Brian was just a funny, outgoing, smart person with a funny sense of humor, you know, but it was cut with intelligence because he was really smart," remembered Andrew Winkel, one of the band of brothers from St. Charles. And "he was somebody who was dedicated to doing good works, to helping other people by living by the Golden Rule."

Andrew and Brian became friends as football teammates

and soon began working on homework together and hanging out on the weekends. It didn't hurt their friendship that Brian had both his license and an "awesome" Pontiac Bonneville, Andrew recalled with laughter — though his driving left a bit to be desired. "One of [Brian's] patented moves was to get on a freeway [and] immediately cut across four lanes into the fast lane just like that was normal. By the way, he did it as safely as one could do it."

Andrew noted, too, that in each of the pictures of their dozen or so friends, Brian was always at the center. "He was a shorter guy so it could have been due to that," Andrew said. "But I think it's more than that. I think he really was the center of our group. And it's still happening today because we still have that bond."

In the months that followed Brian's death, a scholarship fund at St. Charles was established in his name by his father, Charlie, and another scholarship fund was set up at Franciscan University. Both remain active. The football field at Franciscan, where Brian and Chris had played flag football, was renamed Memorial Field. And the tabernacle at Holy Family behind the main altar was donated in his memory. Other monetary gifts went to support Christifideles School.

The generous giving in Brian's name was significant. But his legacy was only just beginning.

8

Cultivating Forgiveness

Then Peter approaching asked him, "Lord, if my brother sins against me, how often must I forgive him? As many as seven times?" Jesus answered, "I say to you, not seven times but seventy-seven times."

— Matthew 18:21–22

What does it mean to forgive? What does it really mean? These were the questions Rachel Muha repeatedly asked herself while working her way through fields in search of her abducted eighteen-year-old son. And they are the questions that charted her path forward after his body was found.

Her friend Martha Favreau had presented her with the challenge to forgive, and Rachel had responded, standing up publicly and stating that she forgave the people who hurt her son before she even knew what they had done.

But forgiveness — real forgiveness — is much more than one statement spoken out loud on one day. It is an act, a choice, a constant and continuous decision to move beyond hatred and the desire for revenge. It is an act, a choice, a constant and continuous decision to choose love.

In his 2020 encyclical on fraternity and social friendship, *Fratelli Tutti*, Pope Francis wrote that forgiveness does not forbid justice but rather demands it. At the same time, he wrote, in demanding justice, one must not succumb to hatred. Though Pope Francis was not elected pope until fourteen years after Brian died, his words on forgiveness originate from the Gospel itself and apply perfectly to Brian's story. Pope Francis wrote:

> The important thing is not to fuel anger, which is unhealthy for our own soul and the soul of our people, or to become obsessed with taking revenge and destroying the other. No one achieves inner peace or returns to a normal life in that way. The truth is that "no family, no group of neighbors, no ethnic group, much less a nation, has a future if the force that unites them, brings them together and resolves their differences is vengeance and hatred. We cannot come to terms and unite for the sake of revenge, or treating others with the same violence with which they treated us, or plotting opportunities for retaliation under apparently legal auspices." Nothing is gained this way and, in the end, everything is lost.

He goes on, acknowledging the great challenge not giving in to anger can be:

> To be sure, "it is no easy task to overcome the bitter legacy of injustices, hostility and mistrust left by conflict. It can only be done by overcoming evil with good (cf. Rom 12:21) and by cultivating those virtues which foster reconciliation, solidarity and peace." In this way, "persons who nourish goodness in their heart find that such goodness leads to a peaceful conscience and to profound joy, even in the midst of difficulties and misunderstandings. Even when affronted, goodness is never weak but rather, shows its strength by refusing to take revenge." Each of us should realize that "even the harsh judgment I hold in my heart against my brother or my sister, the open wound that was never cured, the offense that was never forgiven, the rancour that is only going to hurt me, are all instances of a struggle that I carry within me, a little flame deep in my heart that needs to be extinguished before it turns into a great blaze."*

• • •

In the more than twenty years since the death of her son, Rachel has made a practice of extinguishing the flames of anger and hatred toward those who killed her son that pop up inside of her. As such, she has been modeling what it means to forgive and teaching others how to do the same.

It hasn't been easy. Rachel has had to carefully weigh her decisions and be deliberate about not putting herself into situations where she might be tempted to hate. When it was time for Nathan and Terrell to be formally charged, she didn't go to their arraignments, and she didn't want her family to go either. "I'm not ready to see their faces and not hate them," she admitted to family and friends at the time. Some of her family did

* Pope Francis, *Fratelli Tutti*, par. 242–243, vatican.va.

go, though, and they were furious after seeing the two suspects, knowing that they were the last ones to have seen Brian alive. Rachel was heartbroken, but she was also affirmed. She had the power to set the tone, and she knew she had to use it for good.

"If I was vengeful and hateful, my Chris would be, too, the students would be, family members would be," Rachel said. "It would block any good that God would try to bring out of it. I knew I had to [forgive] for Chris and the rest of my family, and for God to work miracles on Terrell and Nathan," she added. "If they only see hatred from us, they can't see God. You forgive because God asks it of us, and then God takes care of the rest."

At the memorial Mass for Brian and Aaron at Franciscan University, Fr. Augustine Donegan said that because of Rachel's example, the peace of Christ was present among the community as they searched and waited for news of the boys. "We did not experience the cry of vengeance," he said. "The mother who stood up and said, 'I forgive. I forgive the man who took my son's life,' expressed the essence of Christianity."

Forgiveness requires using the grace God gives us every single day to do good and refuse to do bad. Rachel had to refuse to hate. She had to refuse to want revenge. She had to trample on those feelings and destroy them, no matter how strong they were. But, Rachel said, more than turning away from hatred, forgiveness is turning toward grace. It is looking to do God's will — to bring good even to the worst of situations. As the *Catechism of the Catholic Church* states: "It is not in our power not to feel or to forget an offense; but the heart that offers itself to the Holy Spirit turns injury into compassion and purifies the memory in transforming the hurt into intercession" (2843).

"So what good can we do in this situation?" Rachel recalled asking herself. She realized that "the best thing we can do is to pray for those who hurt us. Forgiveness to me meant refusing to hate and doing all we can to see to it that Terrell and Nathan have every chance to get to heaven." This realization brought acceptance. Her suffering wasn't relieved, but she had a path forward.

When Rachel professed her forgiveness of Terrell and Nathan in the chapel on that Thursday night, she saw her father sobbing as she returned to her pew. "I never saw him cry," she said. "And I felt so grateful that I could bring him a little bit of peace because I knew his tears meant he wasn't going to hate. We all hate what they did. But I could honestly say nobody hates them."

• • •

Over the years, Rachel has come up with nine tips, based on her own experience, prayer, and lessons learned, to help others cultivate forgiveness. They are as follows:

1. When something bad happens: Stop. You are in a decisive moment. Consciously, even verbally, choose God. Choose to face the future with God, not without him. He is there for you, pouring out graces for you to accept.
2. When we get a bit of bad news, it is usually just that: a bit. There is usually more to come. Things usually get worse before they get better. To prepare for that: Pray first. Then act. Ask through prayer. Pray for strength. Pray for courage. Pray for patience. Pray for perseverance. Pray to be able to accept. Pray to fight the good fight. These are prayers that God always answers with a "Yes!" Believe he is giving you those things because he is.
3. You are not done praying. Pray until the situation you are in is resolved. Then keep praying: prayers of thanksgiving.

4. Arm yourself with the right prayer. This is one of the times in our lives when a memorized prayer can be the best prayer because our minds are in such distress. So, calm yourself. Be still. Be quiet. Listen to the promptings of God. The situation you are in, or God himself, is probably giving you clues as to which prayer should be your companion-prayer in this situation.
5. If your situation calls for you to forgive: Forgive. Do it now. Forgiveness is an act of the will, not of our feelings. Do it whether you feel like it or not. Say it out loud: "I forgive ________________." Do it again and again. And then guard your heart, mind, and soul: Don't go anywhere, see anyone, do anything that could take away your resolve to forgive. Not yet. You are not ready yet to see someone who has hurt you or someone who would try to take away your resolve. Keep praying.
6. Pray for those who hurt you. Ask God to fill them with a love for him. "Lord, please give ________________ the joy of knowing you. Amen."
7. Forgiving doesn't mean excusing. Don't just brush off bad behavior. That won't help anyone. Our Lord forgave the good thief but he didn't take away his punishment. Forgiveness is real when we say to the offender, "You did something wrong and I forgive you. Let's correct it together."
8. Whenever someone is trying to do God's will, the devil is trying to make them do the opposite. Be ready for the temptations, be alert, stay strong. Don't give in. Think. Reason. Pray. Fight.
9. Turn your grief into giving. Give. Give. Give. I am not speaking of giving money. Give yourself. Give

> your time and attention. Giving is an act of love and love is the antidote to pain, sadness, trouble, and grief. This step is crucial. It heals. This step is not optional. This step heals you, the one who hurt you, the world around you — and beyond. One evil act spreads destruction. One merciful act spreads joy, love and peace. Please don't leave this step out.

Rachel continues to make the choice to forgive every day. But forgiveness doesn't mean she wants her son back any less. And forgiveness doesn't take away pain — nor should we want it to. She continued:

> People have to stop asking God to take away pain. You can ask God to take away cancer or take away some illness you might have. But we need to value pain more. We don't want to inflict it on ourselves. We don't want to inflict it on anybody else and say, "Oh, this is good for you." But when we're in pain, we should use that. It's so precious. It's so valuable. Use it to do good. Offer it up for somebody else — that really does make a difference. If you want to be Christ-like, you have to offer up your pain. Offer it up. That makes your pain worth suffering.

And real forgiveness has an impact on many more than just the individual. "God is not self-focused, and we shouldn't be either," Rachel said. "The gifts he gives us are for everyone who comes in contact with us, and really even everyone who doesn't." She added:

> Imagine if I went through life without that act of forgiveness. I would be angry. I would be tough. I would

> be hardened. I would be afraid to make relationships. The repercussions are enormous and could affect even strangers that I don't know. Forgiveness makes life easier and more peaceful, more Christ-like all the way around. So we're really foolish not to forgive.

• • •

Forgiveness means something different to each person, said Fr. Mick Kelly years later. "But then you see Rachel Muha and you see somebody living at the extreme end of human suffering, forgiving the people who caused it. And you just realize that this needs the life of a hero to be able to do. To be a Christian you need to be made of tougher stuff, better stuff, more loving stuff than anybody else."

That tension makes this story unique, he added. "You don't know which way to feel. Of course you feel sad, and of course you're amazed — why wouldn't you be?" he said. "The senselessness. The brutality. The sheer wicked evil of it all. The mindlessness of the violence. The stupidity of it. The cruelty that [Terrell and Nathan] inflicted on [Brian and Aaron] in their last hours. The total disregard for the dignity of human life. And then this unbelievable witness to the power of grace and forgiveness."

Rachel's brother, Rick, noted that Brian's death could have torn their family apart. But Rachel's example kept them focused on what was really important. "When you keep your mind on the right things — like your religion, like prayers, like forgiveness — when those are the things that are foremost in your mind, it eliminates those other options and they're no longer options. They're not even thoughts," he said.

But not everyone is so sure that forgiveness is the right path. Sometimes people will ask Rachel: "Aren't you lessening the seriousness of what Terrell and Nathan did to Brian by forgiving them?" Rachel believes forgiveness does the opposite. "If you insist on being angry or vengeful, aren't you lessening what it means to be a child of God?" she asked. "So really your forgiveness shows the world that life is so valuable that we can rise to the heights we never dreamed of by an act of forgiveness."

Forgiveness has nothing to do with the other person, she said, and it should be something that we do immediately. "Do it when you don't feel like it. The minute you think you have something to forgive, forgive it, and then forgive it again, and forgive it again, and forgive it again instead of waiting," she said. "What damage are you doing while you're waiting? Who are you talking about? What little gossip are you carrying on? And all the other sins that go with a hard heart. Soften your hearts."

The goal is to get to the point where you can remember to forgive without anger and without vengefulness, she said. Instead, substitute pity for anger. "When somebody sins, we need to feel compassion for them," she said. "We want them out of their sin. We should want to be brothers and sisters together — to walk that path to heaven together."

Chris acknowledges that his mother's example of forgiveness made all the difference for him as they walked this terrible road together. "I can't imagine going through this without her guidance," he said. "I don't know what I would have done without her. I hope I would have reacted the same way, but all I know is I did have her guidance. I'm incredibly fortunate."

At the same time, he understands those who may struggle to forgive after such a heinous act of violence. And he believes that a strong foundation of faith helps one to be able to make the right choices. "It's the little things you have to be building in yourself — your character and virtue and growing in holiness every day in all the little things," Chris said. "That's what makes you ready, I guess, for the big things."

Unfortunately for the Muhas, there were still more big things to come.

Part II

9
Dealing with the Grief

The Lord is close to the brokenhearted,
saves those whose spirit is crushed.

— Psalm 34:19

How does one cope with the loss of a child? It is the nightmare scenario of all parents — the sword of sorrow that pierces the heart of those who are forced to endure the death of the miracle they helped to create. The pain, the agony, and the sadness are all-consuming and can be crippling.

In the weeks, months, and years after Brian's murder, Rachel Muha experienced more than her share of overwhelming grief. That first summer, she went by herself to the cemetery every day, longing to be physically close to the son she had birthed and raised, even though he was now buried in the ground. She went to the grocery store early in the morning to avoid seeing anyone. She felt comfortable only at home or at Mass, especially in the presence of her older — and now only living — son, Chris. Together, they prayed the Divine Mercy Chaplet each day for Terrell Yarbrough and Nathan Herring as they awaited trial, and their hearts ached for their Brian.

But even as she suffered, Rachel took great solace in the knowledge that she wasn't the first mother to experience such tragedy. The Blessed Mother herself had stood at the foot of the cross, watching helplessly as her beloved Son suffered and died, also seemingly for no reason at all.

• • •

Rachel was resolved that her son's death would not be the end of his story. Being murdered at eighteen would not be Brian's legacy. Rachel saw to that in her choices of forgiveness over hatred, beauty over evil, and generosity over selfishness. "Your every act should be done with love," Saint Paul instructed the people of Corinth (see 1 Cor 16:14), and this was how Rachel, slowly but surely, chose to honor her son.

In August, after he and Rachel had spent three months finding solace in each other's company, Chris made the decision to go back to Franciscan University for his junior year. Rachel agreed — provided he called her every day, "because if you don't, I'm there in two hours looking for you." He agreed.

As she began grappling with her grief alone, Rachel worked to surround herself with beauty. That meant flowers — everywhere. "I started to plant gardens in the backyard and just dig in the dirt and haul stuff around and put down stones," Rachel said. "I mean, I just went crazy planting gardens. There were flowers all over the place." It was an intentional choice, a way to crowd out the evil that had been all too present in her mind. And the physical work helped her cope with her sorrow and the emptiness of life without her younger son.

But Rachel did more than work on her landscaping in the summer of 1999. She started taking public steps to bring good out of the unspeakably evil act that had claimed the life of her son and his friend. Less than three months after Brian and Aaron were abducted from 165 McDowell Street in Steubenville, Rachel purchased the corner-lot property. Built in 1916, the four-bedroom, two-bathroom residence had been Brian's "home" for only one night, but Rachel felt the need to conquer evil — as she had done with the flowers — by turning the scene of that crime into a place that worked for good. "I wanted to reclaim it, to give it back to God," Rachel told the *Pittsburgh Post-Gazette* in 2000. "Something horrible happened there, but I felt it also could be something wonderful. I want it to be a beacon for the whole neighborhood."

Rachel had first thought of purchasing the house during the search for the boys. She later determined that even if the boys couldn't have been rescued, maybe the La Belle neighborhood could. The purchase was, in some ways, a foreshadowing of the inner-city work that would dominate the rest of her life.

Though the owner of the house had not been looking to sell, when he discovered that the potential buyer was the mother of one of the slain students, he not only sold the property but sold it for less than market value and included furnishings and appliances. On August 18, 1999, Rachel purchased the property for $47,000 and named it Divine Mercy House.

Under her supervision, the house was painted, and repairs were made. The second floor was rented out to a local business to help cover the mortgage, and the two-bedroom apartment on the first floor, from which Brian and Aaron had been abducted, became housing available for priests or consecrated men and women in need of a place to stay while at Franciscan.

The following summer, two priests from Africa moved in. Their "rent"? To pray and offer Mass for Brian and Aaron, their families and friends, Terrell and Nathan, and the whole neighborhood. "Such evil happened here, now nothing but good things can happen," Rachel told the Associated Press. "My wish is to have Mass celebrated every day there." This free housing option was also a gift to the university that had been so attentive during the search for and discovery of Brian and Aaron.

"We keep our tuition costs as low as possible, but it can still be a stretch," Lisa Ferguson, spokeswoman for Franciscan University at the time of the sale, said to the *Post-Gazette*. "For priests from Africa and Third World countries, it can be especially difficult. So what [Muha] has done is a great boon for them. I have met few people who are so inspiring." Divine Mercy House has since become available to low-income students at Franciscan as well as religious.

The purchase did not come without sacrifice for Rachel. Though she scraped the down payment together through the generosity of thirty-five of her cousins, Rachel had to take out another twenty-year mortgage and a home-equity loan on her own home. Years later, when the state reconfigured Route 22, the commemorative cross that had stood at the site of the slayings in Washington County was moved back to Steubenville to stand guard in the front yard of the house from which the boys had been taken, and which Rachel now owned.

But purchasing the home did not lift Rachel out of her misery. Month after month, more than anything, she continued to want her son back, alive and in her arms. When she told a friend just that, however, the friend responded: "You don't want him back, Rachel." Though Rachel was stunned and stung, her friend continued: "Brian, knowing what he knows now, would choose that terrible death again to get to where he is."

"I wanted to say to her, 'Shut up,' but I didn't," Rachel recalled. "She was so right, and I needed to hear it. You need to be sometimes shaken out of your grief, and she did that for me. I remember her words twenty years later."

About six months after Brian's death, Fr. Kevin Lutz, Rachel's pastor at Holy Family Church in Columbus, asked Rachel if she would be interested in sharing Brian's story with an ecumenical group that met monthly for fellowship and instruction. "No," she responded quickly. She couldn't possibly. "That's a shame," he answered back. "Because I already told them you would."

Upset, Rachel looked at the man who had been there for her when Brian was missing and when he was found. He had celebrated Brian's funeral Mass. Brian had loved him. How could she tell him no? She went home, sat down, and, feeling an outpouring of the Holy Spirit, wrote out the whole story. "It deserved to be written down, and so I wrote it. And I spoke it to that group and have been speaking ever since," Rachel said. "Father knew."

It was around this same time that Rachel finally brought herself to look at Nathan and Terrell's mug shots in the newspaper. "I just remember this intense sadness when I saw their faces," she said. "Their faces looked so empty to me, so lifeless, and I remember thinking, 'Really, they're the ones right now, in the condition that they're in, who have lost their lives.' And I just felt so sad."

Back in Steubenville, the La Belle community began a neighborhood watch program called La Belle Neighbors Who Care, which is still in operation today. On Franciscan's campus, Chris found solace both in remembering his brother and in praying for those who had hurt Brian. During weekly gatherings, students gathered for prayer and to share memories of Brian and Aaron, laughing and crying together. They also went to Divine Mercy House for Mass and out to the hill where Brian and Aaron died.

• • •

On Mother's Day of 2000, almost a year after Brian was killed, Rachel wrote a long letter to family and friends talking about the process of grief and describing her experience of the past year — what she called "a year of the longest, slowest days you could ever imagine":

> A year of knowing that the son and brother you love so much will never come through the door again — will never sit across from you at dinner — will never again say "I'm coming" after you have tried to wake him up three times. A year without hugging him good morning and good night — and good-bye. A year of sad drives to the cemetery — of dreading the turn into its road, of winding around and parking the car and walking up to the gravestone that has my son's name on it. Of needing to be close to Brian — but being so far away. A year of watching Chris, so young, be so strong — and admiring him, while my heart breaks for him.

Rachel wrote of how she learned in that first terrible year after her son's murder that she and her family and friends were not actually living without Brian — because Brian, though gone physically from the world, had remained an active part of their lives:

> Love is stronger than death, and those that have died are closer to us now, love us more, than they ever did, and more than we are capable of loving them. God knows the longing of a mother's heart because it is the same longing of his heart — to be with your children. God wouldn't let death cut us off from Brian — that would be a cruel god, not a loving Father. So even now, we can

> be with Brian, talk to him and "feel" his presence. He can be with us — and he wants to be! And he can help us.

During that first year, many people told Rachel that they were praying for and to Brian, and it was not uncommon for her to hear stories of how Brian had helped people at certain times. A neighbor shared with her that when he had been working at a fast-food restaurant late at night, three masked robbers had entered. Angry at how little money was on the premises, one of the robbers put a gun to the neighbor's head, and another told him to pull the trigger. All the neighbor could think was "Brian, Brian, Brian." "He looked at the hand that was holding the gun, and he thought for sure he would die," Rachel recalled. "But the robber hesitated and his hand started to shake. Then he just ran. The other two followed."

Another story was related by a pro-life doctor in the Columbus area who was counseling a young couple determined to terminate a pregnancy. After talking to them for an hour and a half and making no progress, the doctor prayed, "Brian, you wanted to be a doctor. I'm a doctor. Help me!" In that moment, the doctor related, he got the idea to talk about the Visitation — how the baby in Elizabeth's womb leapt at the sound of Mary's voice because he knew that Jesus — in Mary's womb — was alive and nearby. The couple decided to keep the baby. It is fitting that this reported intercession on Brian's part is tied to the Visitation, since it was on the feast of the Visitation that he died.

• • •

As part of her grieving process, Rachel communicated regularly with her family via email. Sometimes these notes contained updates about the trials or other information about the case. But more often than not they were spiritual musings — a way for her to impart the lessons she was learning about loss, suffering, and faith to those around her. The emailed letters provided opportunity after opportunity for deepening the faith of those who loved Brian and for bringing souls closer to God. In particular, Rachel shared in several emails, starting in December 1999, her reflections on the book, *The Happiness of Heaven*, by Fr. F. J. Boudreaux, SJ.

"The Beatific Vision in its amazing sweetness is this: God enables a soul to see Him in all His wondrous beauty *and also takes that soul to Himself as a beloved child and bestows upon it the happiness which mortal eyes cannot see*," Rachel wrote (emphasis her own). She continued:

> Picture a mother holding her infant close to her heart. The baby is filled with confidence, peace and contentment. You can see it on his little face. There is no sweeter picture of love than this. Can there be a more beautiful image of Heaven? Not to a mother whose heart breaks and arms ache to hold her son again. Knowing that our Brian is so welcomed by God and held tight — knowing that Brian's pain, fear and anguish was wiped away and replaced with everlasting joy, peace, and deep love — knowing that Bri *knows without a doubt* how much he is loved by God — what else could I want to know? Tears come as I write this — out of love for God for loving Bri so much; out of gratitude to God for loving Bri; out of a strong and I know perpetual desire to be with Bri in such a beautiful place; out of a deep desire that we all get there *soon*; out of a fear of losing such an eternity. Still, the longing for Bri continues.

Though it eased over time, that longing would never go away. And throughout that first year, as Rachel worked through her grief and sought out ways to keep Brian's memory alive, she knew she still had to face the trials of those who had killed him.

10

The First Trial: Nathan Herring

You have been told, O mortal, what is good,
and what the Lord *requires of you:*
Only to do justice and to love goodness,
and to walk humbly with your God.

— *Micah 6:8*

About fifteen months after the kidnapping and murder of Brian Muha and Aaron Land, Nathan Herring and Terrell Yarbrough stood trial, separately, at the Jefferson County Courthouse in Steubenville, Ohio.

Delay after delay — including for psychiatric evaluations,

for forensic analysis, for holidays, and in an abundance of caution to avoid any chance of a mistrial — had postponed the trials. But Nathan Herring's trial finally began with jury selection on August 16, 2000, followed by opening statements on August 21. Terrell Yarbrough's was scheduled for a month later. Each trial, including jury selection and sentencing, lasted approximately two weeks.

Rachel and Chris were anxious. In early August, Rachel had asked that friends and family "storm heaven" to pray for wisdom for the judge and jury, for all the attorneys in their pursuit of justice, for the conversions of Terrell and Nathan, and for mercy on everyone. She asked for the prayers of various prayer groups and religious orders, and that children pray for a "special intention."

For Chris, being in the courtroom was surreal. He felt somewhat detached — wondering, on some level, what he was even doing there. He worried about how difficult it would be for Rachel to see Nathan and Terrell in person for the first time. He also worried that justice might not be served. He was angry at the character witnesses and at the psychologist who were brought in to claim that the suspects weren't really responsible for their actions given the circumstances of their upbringings. Chris feared the young men might literally get away with murder on a technicality.

Chris also had a desire to confront Nathan and Terrell — not in an aggressive way, but in a way that would help them understand that they never had any real power over Brian at the time of his death. He wanted them to know that he and the rest of Brian's family were there to join the justice system in holding them accountable for their actions. "I wanted to show them that we knew what they did, and that no one was going to let them get away with it," Chris said — but that at the same time, what they did wasn't the end of the story. The family wanted more for them than punishment, but it had to begin with an acknowledgment of wrongdoing.

• • •

In his opening statement for Nathan's trial, with photos and videotape of Brian and Aaron's bodies showing on a screen, Jefferson County Prosecutor Stephen Stern told jurors: "They went to bed expecting to get up and enjoy the Memorial Day holiday like everyone else. At 5:45 a.m., they were dead. They were lying dead on a hillside in a marsh, covered with maggots."

As Nathan's trial unfolded, evidence against him began to pile up. Over the next four days, the prosecution called a number of witnesses, the first of which was Andrew Doran, Brian and Aaron's roommate, who testified that he had awakened to noise, escaped through his bedroom window, and run to a neighbor's house and called the police. Barbara Vey identified Nathan as one of the two men who had grabbed her outside of her Pittsburgh apartment and stolen her green BMW on May 31, 1999. She testified that they had pointed a gun at her and threatened to pull the trigger if she didn't give them her car keys. Steubenville police detectives John Lelless and Sgt. Charles Sloane testified to their findings as they worked the case, including the discovery of Brian's credit and ATM cards in Nathan's residence. In addition, tape recordings of both Terrell and Nathan were played; when detained and questioned during the search for Brian and Aaron, each had blamed the other for the crimes.

Forensic pathologist Dr. Leon Rozin of Allegheny County, Pennsylvania, who performed the autopsies on Brian and Aaron, described the condition of the bodies when they were found on June 4, 1999: decomposed and covered with weeds and maggots. He determined that gunshots to the head had been the cause of death for both victims, adding that studying Brian's head had been difficult because of the disfigurement of his body. "It looked like he was beheaded," Rozin said. "The naked spine was visible at the top of the body. All the soft tissue was gone and there was no brain. There was a hole right behind the right ear." Rozin had removed a bullet from Brian's spine, but there was no bullet found for Aaron. The nature of the wounds, according to his testimony, suggested that the perpetrators had pressed the gun against the victims' heads. He also testified that the jaws of both victims were broken, detached from the skull with multiple fractures; these injuries were caused, he said, "by another trauma and not the gunshot." No drugs had been found in their systems, he also confirmed.

Other key witnesses included DNA analysis expert Julie Kidd from the FBI crime labs in Washington, DC, who testified that Nathan's blood had been found in the Blazer, in Barbara Vey's BMW, on his own jacket, and on the receipt generated by the ATM machine when Nathan and Terrell attempted to use Brian's debit card to get cash. Nathan's fingerprints were also found in the Blazer and on the ATM receipt. And FBI forensic scientists, including Charles Peters, testified that the bullets used in the murders of Brian and Aaron matched the .44-caliber Magnum ammunition found in Nathan Herring's home.

The goal of Nathan's defense attorney, David Doughten, was to show that his defendant was not the principal offender (i.e., the one who had pulled the trigger). That role, he said, had belonged to Terrell. Doughten brought several witnesses to the stand to testify that Terrell had bragged about committing the murders. Brandon Young testified that Terrell had given him a ride in the Blazer later in the day on May 31. "He said he killed two white boys," Brandon said. Terrell himself took the stand briefly, during which time he plead the Fifth and offered no other comment.

In his endeavor to convince the jury that Nathan was not the principal offender, Doughten was successful. On Friday, August 25, after nearly four days of testimony and approximately ten hours of deliberations, the jury found Nathan guilty of twelve counts of aggravated murder in connection with Brian and Aaron's deaths; two counts of aggravated robbery and kidnapping with firearm specifications; and one count each of aggravated burglary, receiving stolen property, and grand theft auto for the Chevy Blazer. The jury also found that the murders had been precalculated, in the course of a felony, and in an attempt to avoid detection, apprehension, trial, and punishment. Jurors ruled, however, that Nathan was not the principal offender.

During the sentencing phase of the trial, which began the following Tuesday, August 29, the defense team brought forward family, friends, and other witnesses to talk about Nathan's life and circumstances in the hope that the jury could be persuaded to recommend a sentence of life imprisonment over the death penalty.

In his testimony, John Angelotta, a clinical counselor specializing in substance abuse, described how Herring had been surrounded by drug use his entire life: "His parents were chronic users. … The guy grew up in a family using drugs left and right." The death of Nathan's brother, Derrick, was also brought up, as well as the eighth-grade sports injury two years later that forced Nathan to the sidelines and, in his mind, ended any possibility of advancement.

In unsworn testimony, Nathan offered an emotional apology to the families of the victims. "I can only say, I know in a certain situation such as this, apologies ain't going to get it. Sorry ain't going to do it. But I am so terribly sorry. I would like to send my sympathies out. If I could turn back the hands of time …" Nathan broke off, apparently too emotional to continue.

As Rachel listened to the witnesses, she was struck by the difficulty of the lives that Terrell and Nathan had lived. It didn't excuse what they had done, but it touched Rachel's heart in a way that would stay with her. "They're eighteen years old," Rachel said in a recent interview. "They know that there's a law against murder. But they don't know why. They don't value life because nobody valued theirs."

There were kids growing up like Terrell and Nathan all over the world, all over the country, and in downtown Columbus, she realized. "What am I doing about it?" she asked herself. "How guilty am I for what happened to Brian?" Years later, Rachel reflected further on that point. "I think we all are guilty," she said. "We all have to accept that, or we won't change it, you know? It's a whole value of life. I remember Mother Teresa saying abortion is going to lead to nuclear war, and people would say, 'What is she talking about?' But she's so right. If you don't value life at the beginning, you're not going to value it ever, and we're seeing that."

On Wednesday, August 30, after more than five hours of deliberation, the jury recommended that Nathan be sentenced to life in prison without parole. Common Pleas Judge Joseph J. Bruzzese Jr. then sentenced Herring to two life terms (one per victim) without parole for the murders, plus an additional sixty-five years for other charges.

• • •

Before Nathan was escorted from the courtroom, family members of the victims were invited to speak. This was the only time they were permitted to address the court or the defendant, and they made the most of the opportunity.

Charlie, Brian's father, reflected on how he was filled with "an overwhelming sense of pain and sadness" at the loss of his son:

> As a parent, my worst nightmare, my worst nightmare was always going to be a call in the middle of the night saying, "Your son's been killed in an automobile accident." Never in my wildest and darkest moments would

> I ever envision a gruesome, horrific set of events leading to Brian's death. … This will never make any sense. We'll never be able to understand how you could do this to two people for no reason.

Chris spoke to Nathan of the memories of times with Brian that he cherished, telling him that he understood Nathan's pain at losing his own brother because now Chris had lost his. But, he said:

> It is because of you that this has happened. It is because of you that I have lost my brother, that I am going through what you went through. You have admitted to being responsible for the murder of my brother. I will hardly be able to think of Brian without thinking of you. You have become forever associated with him for me. I cannot help but see him when I see you, think of him when I think of you. Whether I like it or not, you are one of the closest links I now have to my brother. You were the last person to see him alive. In a very real way, my memory of my brother will always be attached to you.

"My brother and your brother are gone," Chris went on. "God willing, they are both in heaven. God willing, they are brothers now. All that remains is for you and I to become brothers. You cannot turn back the hands of time like you said, but you can do the next best thing. You can become like my brother was." In order to do that, Chris said, Nathan had to truly be sorry for his actions and accept his punishment. "It's only by becoming good that you can turn back the hands of time and give me back my brother, as much as that is possible," he concluded.

In her own moving address, Rachel shared the story of St. Maria Goretti, who was assaulted, stabbed, and murdered by eighteen-year-old Alessandro Serenelli in Italy in 1902. Before she died, Maria forgave Alessandro. Years later, Maria appeared to Alessandro in prison, and he came to know that she had been praying for him. He finally owned up to his crime, repented for what he had done, and changed his life.

"He realized, Nathan, that his best friend turned out to be the person that he killed because she cared about the life he would have after his death," Rachel said. "That's a real friend. Your best friends, Nathan, are in heaven now, and their names are Brian and Aaron."

In her long, heartfelt talk, Rachel encouraged Nathan to admit what he had done, seek forgiveness, and change his ways — or face the ultimate consequence: hell. "In hell you will see all that God has done for you while you were on this earth and how you spit in his face," Rachel said. "In hell you will wish you could die to avoid the pain, but you can't. I don't want you to go to hell, Nathan. … I'm praying for you." (The full version of Rachel's and Chris's victim statements can be found in Appendix A.)

The only reaction Chris and Rachel got from Nathan was during Chris's speech, when he spoke about their two lost brothers. It wasn't much, but it was something. When the trial concluded, Nathan was handcuffed and sent to prison to begin serving his life sentence.

11

Racial Tensions and the Death Penalty

Be kind to one another, compassionate, forgiving one another as God has forgiven you in Christ.

— Ephesians 4:32

As if having to grieve the death of a child and a sibling — the suffering from which is compounded exponentially by torture and murder — wasn't enough to handle, Rachel and Chris also had to navigate the related challenges of racial tensions and questions about the death penalty in the wake of Brian's death. With white victims, Black perpetrators, and extensive national media coverage of the case, it was nearly impossible for racial friction to be avoided. And almost as soon as Brian and Aaron were found murdered on that Pennsylvania hill, speculation about whether the death penalty should be sought — or was warranted — began to swirl within the Steubenville community and beyond. These complications only elevated an already high-profile double murder and, for Rachel's family, made living through the loss of Brian all the more difficult.

• • •

In July 1999, just weeks after the bodies of Brian and Aaron were found, members of the Ku Klux Klan rallied in Steubenville in protest of the killings of the students. "White power, white power," one member chanted into a microphone. Another said: "We are here because of the two white boys that got killed. Justice has to be done."

Organized by the American Knights of the KKK out of the village of Old Washington, Ohio, the rally was held on the steps of the Jefferson County Courthouse on a Saturday afternoon. Community, church, and political leaders called on people to "combat this hate group" by not attending the rally, and the Steubenville branch of the National Association for the Advancement of Colored People (NAACP) held alternative events — a family picnic, free swimming at area parks, and the like — to deter people from going to the rally to counterprotest. Steubenville Councilman Jim Fox, who also worked in public relations for Franciscan University at the time, said the university was appalled by the KKK gathering. "We think it's disgusting that [the Klan] would use the deaths of our students as an excuse to hold this rally," Fox said.

The KKK rally, though peaceful, signaled the undercurrent of racial tension that inevitably arises with cases of violent crime involving different races. This is especially true in eastern Ohio, where racial disparities are stark. As the trials approached, suggestions that one race was "after" the other swelled in the media and in the Steubenville community.

Questions of race arose again on the first day of the trial of Nathan Herring. On Monday, August 21, the NAACP issued a statement in which they took umbrage at the racial makeup of the jury, which was comprised of nine white women, two white men, and one Native American man. Chief Deputy Prosecuting Attorney Chris Becker downplayed the absence of Black people on the jury, saying that he believed the jury had been chosen fairly.

Watching carefully was Tony Norman, a Black columnist for the *Pittsburgh Post-Gazette*, who wrote in early September 2000 that following the deaths of two white boys at the hands of two Black boys, he had been "convinced that the region's simmering racial tensions were about to be stoked." But then came Nathan's trial and the victim statements. "I never expected eloquent speeches about forgiveness and redemption to fill the courtroom," Norman wrote. "From [Nathan's] own family, I expected sympathy, but not from the families of his victims." He identified Rachel's statement as "a gracious speech [that] will reverberate for years in that sad and divided community."

"[Nathan] had no idea a year ago that he'd ever be confronted by such a woman," according to Norman. "Had he known such love in his life, he would've wrestled his partner to the ground. Taking a bullet would've been better than living under the weight of a heartbroken mother's prayers."

"Rachel Muha's redemption song has stunned and inspired many people," Norman continued. "What the petite woman did in the presence of the tall man who helped kill her son required a bravery beyond what it takes to squeeze the trigger of a gun. What good is hatred? Rachel Muha understands that, sometimes, the language of redemption is the only thing in the whole world that makes any sense."

In his victim statement at the trial of Terrell Yarbrough, Chris Muha shared his incredulity about some of the racially charged comments he had been hearing:

> I heard someone earlier this week saying Terrell hadn't been given a fair trial; that he didn't have a jury of his peers. I heard the same thing expressed in the newspaper by someone from the local NAACP just before Nathan Herring's trial. The person who made that statement explained what she meant by it: Nathan's jury was all white. His peers, the only ones who could judge him fairly, were Blacks. Do we realize what is being said here?! Does this not promote the idea of "separate but equal" that Blacks fought so hard to abolish some forty years ago? If the only ones who can judge Terrell honestly are Black people, what does that say about the races? It says we are so different as to be unable to relate to each other. We are separate, but equal. Martin Luther King Jr. would shake his head in dismay if he were here witnessing members of his own race destroying what he fought so hard to abolish. …
>
> I want you to know, Terrell, that when Brian looked at you that early morning, he saw the hate in your eyes, he saw the viciousness in your face, but I know he didn't see the color of your skin. He didn't care about skin color. … He didn't hate people because of their skin color — he didn't hate anyone.

For Rachel, race was a nonissue from the start. "None of us thought about it until it was brought up on some radio shows in Steubenville," she said. "Not one person [in our family] said, 'Oh, [the killers] were Black.' It was two young boys who killed two young boys."

• • •

Under Ohio law, the charges facing Terrell and Nathan made them both eligible for the death penalty, and from the beginning of the case, Jefferson County Prosecutor Stephen Stern said that if he ended up leading the prosecution, he would seek capital punishment for both suspects.

The death penalty ranks as one of most controversial social issues in the United States. In 2021, according to a Gallup poll, only 54 percent of Americans were in favor of capital punishment for a person convicted of murder. But at the turn of the new millennium, public opinion was quite a bit different. The same Gallup poll taken in February 1999 — just three and a half months before Brian and Aaron were murdered — found that 71 percent of Americans favored the death penalty for a murder convict. Rachel, as a woman of deep faith, was determined to follow the teaching of the Catholic Church as she established her personal position on whether or not Terrell and Nathan should receive the death penalty.

The position of the Catholic Church on the death penalty reflects both Scripture and the Church's Tradition, which have been interpreted and applied over the millennia according to circumstances of the time. In 2018, Pope Francis, declaring capital punishment to be "inadmissible because it is an attack on the inviolability and dignity of the person," amended paragraph 2267 of the *Catechism* to reflect this interpretation of Church teaching. The new entry adds that the Church "works with determination for [the death penalty's] abolition worldwide."

But prior to 2018, the Church offered a more nuanced approach, relying heavily upon the teaching of Pope John Paul II in his encyclical *Evangelium Vitae* ("The Gospel of Life"). In 1999, the *Catechism* stated:

> Assuming that the guilty party's identity and responsibility have been fully determined, the traditional teaching of the Church does not exclude recourse to the death penalty, if this is the only possible way of effectively defending human lives against the unjust aggressor.
>
> If, however, non-lethal means are sufficient to defend and protect people's safety from the aggressor, authority will limit itself to such means, as these are more in keeping with the concrete conditions of the common good and more in conformity with the dignity of the human person.
>
> Today, in fact, as a consequence of the possibilities which the state has for effectively preventing crime, by rendering one who has committed an offense incapable of doing harm — without definitively taking away from him the possibility of redeeming himself — the cases in which the execution of the offender is an absolute necessity "are very rare, if not practically nonexistent." (2267)

In short, while the Church tolerated capital punishment at the time, it was only to be applied when it was necessary to protect life.

• • •

From the beginning of this horrible ordeal, Rachel was clear in her dislike of the death penalty. In the November 28, 1999, issue of the *Catholic Times*, the newspaper of the Diocese of Columbus, Rachel published an essay titled "I Don't Want My Son's Killers Put to Death." In it, she recounted the terrible details of what had happened to Brian, writing, "If ever there was a 'right' to expect — to demand — the death penalty for someone, it would be our right to demand it." But Rachel didn't want to do that, she wrote, because "each of us was created, and we were created for heaven." She went on:

> Our Creator had one purpose in mind when he fashioned our souls: to live with him forever in eternal happiness, with no more suffering. That is our Creator's purpose, and we, his creatures, have no right to deny one of our brothers or sisters every chance possible to do just that: to save his or her soul.
>
> How has our heavenly Father ordained it so we can do that? He gives us graces in great abundance — and he gives us time. With that time we make choices; we commit sins; we turn away from God — and turn back to him for forgiveness and help. When time runs out, we are judged and sentenced: eternal misery or eternal joy.
>
> That is the ultimate reason no one has the right to kill. The killers who took Brian's and Aaron's time away from them didn't know or care if they were sentencing the boys to eternal bliss or eternal damnation. They didn't care at all about the state of the boys' souls. ...
>
> Rejection of the death penalty does not mean rejection of justice or punishment. If we excuse them, we offer them no real hope for a life of happiness. We have to have real love for them — a love that requires accountability and demands conversion.
>
> It is very hard to love someone who hurt your son — very hard. God asks a lot of us — and he asks that. So we must do it.
>
> Real compassion begins with forgiveness, but also says: I know what you did. You were wrong — you were bad. But together we can become holy.

As the trials approached in the late summer of 2000, Rachel addressed the death penalty with her friends and family via email; in the course of the letter, she wrote of the tension between justice and mercy:

> If we want a safe society and we truly want to reform criminals, the Church teaches that we should show mercy. Mercy is a kindness undeserved. The Church is saying that yes, the criminal deserves death, but try undeserved kindness and see what effect it has on the world.
>
> Now, you cannot have mercy without justice. Justice still demands to be satisfied, even though we are called to be merciful. So, how do we meet all the requirements? We look at justice in a new way, maybe a deeper way.
>
> To me, justice is not saying, "You caused Brian and Aaron, and thousands of others, great pain and suffering, now we are entitled to cause you great pain and suffering. To me, justice is not saying, "You killed — now I am going to kill." The scales of justice are tipped when an unjust act is committed. If an ineffective act is committed to punish the first act, the scales are not righted, they are tipped even more and soon the whole balance falls over.
>
> To me, justice is saying, "You caused so much pain and suffering, now you have to alleviate it." "You took two souls out of this world who would have done much good, now you have to replace the good you took"; "You have caused some people to lose faith in God! Now you have to become pillars of faith"; "You have made some people have to fight feelings of prejudice. Now you have to show love to all peoples." And I could go on and on. But do you see? That is the only way justice is restored, and Brian and Aaron are justified. You see, when the

> bad guys can honestly say, "I want to be like Brian and Aaron," I will know "justice was served" — I will know God won.
>
> In my opinion, when someone takes an innocent life, the punishment has to be stiff and uncompromising: It has to be life in prison without parole. If [Nathan and Terrell] can accept their punishment and live out their lives in prison meekly, then a lot of good will be restored.

Fr. Mick Kelly, the one-time Franciscan student, now priest of the Diocese of Arlington, said that Rachel's lesson on forgiveness and justice affected him profoundly:

> As a Catholic, it makes sense. We never leave the confessional without a penance. It's not that God lets us off the hook, but he actually asks us to collaborate in repenting of our evil, which means restoring justice, in some sense, to what we've done wrong.
>
> It's such a simple idea. It should be so easy to communicate, and it's one of the hardest things people really come to terms with, with Christianity. They don't get that. They really expect God to let you off the hook. But what a terrible God he would be, where evil doesn't matter, and there's no restoration of justice and no restoration of things that are lost.

Despite her conviction, Rachel did admit that she was struggling with very strong feelings of anger, and to get through them she needed to rely on God more than ever. She wrote to her family:

> Left to myself, I know I could easily seek more than the death penalty — I could seek pain and suffering for the

> bad guys. … Left to myself, I could hate them. Left to myself, I could kill them. And then I would be left to myself — without my Brian, or my Chris, or my God. Forever. So I, clinging to our God, will not let the bad guys do that. Not to me, not to Chris — I hope not to any of you. They took two precious lives — we will not give them any more. When feelings of revenge and anger get stirred up, trample on them with an act of your will — "For me and my house, we will serve the Lord."

In September 2000, however, more information surfaced. It came out during the trials that Terrell had attacked three people in prison in recent months, that he was threatening others, and that he had helped one inmate try to hang himself (unsuccessfully). From the very beginning, Rachel had made it clear that she wanted Terrell and Nathan never to be a danger to another soul again. After consulting with several priests and the prison officials, who said Terrell wouldn't last long in the general population, she determined that she would not oppose the death penalty in Terrell's case as she had in Nathan's. Sending Terrell to death row, she and Chris determined, was the best way not only to keep others safe but to keep Terrell safe.

"We were in an awful situation," Rachel said in an interview with the *Catholic Times* later that fall. "We were trying to protect the life of the boy who took Brian's life. Terrell's own lawyers had a psychologist who said that he is a classic sociopath. … We felt he's going to hurt somebody and in the process get hurt himself — maybe killed."

On death row, Terrell would be removed from the general population in the prison and be placed in solitary confinement. There, Rachel prayed, he would use his time to stay safe, not be a danger to others, and repent of his crimes. In most cases, Rachel reiterated at the time, the death penalty should not be an option.

But Terrell had proved himself to be a dangerous exception to the rule.

12

The First Trial: Terrell Yarbrough

In just the same way, I tell you, there will be rejoicing among the angels of God over one sinner who repents.

— Luke 15:10

Ahead of Nathan's and Terrell's trials in the late summer and fall of 2000, Rachel Muha spent time reflecting on the story of the prodigal son in Luke's Gospel. In the fifteenth chapter, Luke recounts Jesus' story about a man with two sons, the younger of whom asks his father for his share of the inheritance in advance of his father's death so that he might leave and make his way in the world.

When the father complies, the younger son leaves to begin living a life of sin, eventually squandering his fortune. Starving and out of money, the son begins working for a man, tending to his pigs. After a time, he comes to his senses, and realizes he should go back home and apologize to his father. He thinks: "I shall get up and go to my father and I shall say to him, 'Father, I have sinned against heaven and against you. I no longer deserve to be called your son; treat me as you would treat one of your hired workers'" (vv. 18–19).

While the younger son is still far off, his father spots him in the distance, is filled with compassion, and runs to him and kisses him. Brushing aside his son's profuse apology, the father orders new clothes for his son and commands his servants to slaughter the fattened calf. "Then let us celebrate with a feast," the father says, "because this son of mine was dead, and has come to life again; he was lost, and has been found" (vv. 23–24).

This father's great and loving mercy, as Rachel reminded her family and friends, is the same mercy of our Father in heaven. And the son's admission of guilt and his repentance are fitting justice. Rachel outlined for those who loved Brian Muha what the parable meant for them on the eve of the trials of those who had killed him, embracing the dual call for justice and mercy. She wrote in an email:

> First, we are commanded to forgive, so we do it. Second, we are required to pray for, hope for, sacrifice for, and wait for the bad guys' conversion. Third, real love means recognizing the need for punishment and not standing in its way. Fourth, their recognition that they deserve to be punished for the rest of their lives, and their willingness to be punished — as a matter of fact, their demand that they be punished because they took two innocent lives — will be the sure sign of a repentant person.

"I know that is asking a lot but God can do it," Rachel wrote. "Justice will then demand that they serve their full term — and I would fight for that. Mercy would demand that we do all we can to see to it that their jail cells become their way to Heaven. And I am committed to that. I hope you all are, too."

This commitment to justice and mercy ended up being critical for the Muhas going into Terrell's trial, especially. It soon became clear that, though the courtroom and judge were the same, this trial was going to be quite different from Nathan's. The defendant's family was much more vocal and contentious, and this made the atmosphere all the more challenging for Rachel and her family.

• • •

Jury selection in Terrell Yarbrough's trial began on Wednesday, September 13, 2000, with opening statements following on Monday, September 18. As Nathan had been, Terrell was charged with two counts of aggravated robbery and kidnapping; single counts of aggravated burglary, receiving stolen property, and grand theft auto; and twelve counts of aggravated murder, with death penalty specification.

The testimony lasted three and a half days. During opening statements, Terrell held his head in his hands and appeared to be softly crying. Much of the evidence brought by prosecutors was similar to that in Nathan's trial, though some was unique — and of Terrell's own doing.

"Terrell Yarbrough's urge to tell his friends about what he did to the two university boys was uncontrollable," said Prosecutor Stephen Stern in his opening statement to the jury, which was composed of eight women and four men. "You'll see the more he talks, the deeper he gets himself into a hole."

For their part, the court-appointed defense attorneys, led by

Peter Olivito and Francesca Carinci, tried to paint Terrell as a "decent human being," an "outsider" who got caught up with a bad Steubenville crowd. "He's not very educated. He's not very sophisticated. He's not very well cared for," Olivito said. "He hooked up with a Steubenville crowd that did some things most people wouldn't." It was Nathan, not Terrell, who was the leader, Olivito asserted.

Many of the witnesses who took the stand at Nathan's trial were back for Terrell's, including Andrew Doran, Julie Kidd, Detective John Lelless, Dr. Leon Rozin, Barbara Vey, and Brandon Young.

Other notable witnesses included Brian Porter, a traveler going west on Route 22 who identified Terrell as the driver of the Chevy Blazer he had stopped to help on May 31, 1999. Porter reported that Terrell explained he'd run out of gas, and Porter gave him a lift to a gas station and then back to his car. Terrell's fellow prisoner James Jones testified that Terrell had "bragged" about killing Brian and Aaron and trying to make the crime look drug related. "He said he shot the one kid. He saw the bullet and blood exit the other side," Jones said. And Shawn Dudley of Steubenville related that he had run into Terrell at a car wash on the day of the murders and had noticed blood on his shirt. After Dudley was arrested for possession of cocaine a couple of days later, he said, Terrell told him in prison that he'd shot both Brian and Aaron in the head.

The defense offered one witness: a DNA analyst from a lab in Michigan who challenged the findings of the FBI forensic examiner.

Much of what jurors heard was from Terrell himself, via conflicting statements recorded by Steubenville police when Terrell was detained for questioning after he had been apprehended driving the Blazer on the evening of May 31. His name was Michael Poole, Terrell claimed. He was from New York. Yes, he had been apprehended getting out of the Blazer, but only after Nathan Herring and Brandon Young offered him a ride. He didn't know where the Blazer came from, and he knew nothing about what had happened to Brian and Aaron.

Terrell had stuck with some version of that story until he got word that Nathan and Brandon were talking — and that their talk implicated him. Then, Terrell said it was they who had committed the heinous crimes. It was Nathan who had made plans to rob and kill the students; Terrell was an unarmed lookout.

After three and a half days of testimony, jurors began their deliberations on Thursday afternoon, September 21, 2000. Their discussion was interrupted thirty minutes in when members of Terrell's family and friends claimed they had seen jurors talking with "a relative of Muha." Common Pleas Judge Joseph J. Bruzzese Jr. quizzed Yarbrough's relatives about what they had seen, and then did the same with members of the jury. Based upon his findings, Judge Bruzzese denied the defense's request for a mistrial, telling attorneys that he believed there had been no misconduct. The jury resumed its deliberations for the rest of the evening before being dismissed. The next day, Friday, September 22, the jury reached a verdict at 10:40 a.m., finding Terrell guilty of twelve counts of aggravated murder, as well as kidnapping, aggravated robbery, aggravated burglary, and other crimes. They also ruled that he had been the principal offender — the one to pull the trigger — and that he had planned to commit his crimes and did so in an effort to escape arrest and punishment.

• • •

At the penalty phase of the trial, which began on Tuesday, September 26, jurors listened to testimony from Terrell's family and friends as they attempted to save the defendant's life, even as prosecutors pushed for the ultimate punishment. "There are certain heinous crimes where a jury should evaluate the death penalty," Stern told the *Pittsburgh Post-Gazette*. "If this is not that case, I don't know what is."

Members of Terrell's family and his friends, as well as a psychologist, attempted to dissuade the judge from handing down the death penalty. "Terrell is not a monster," said defense attorney Francesca Carinci. "He started out an innocent baby, just like we all did, but we were lucky to have people who cared for us. He is here today because everyone in his life failed him. You must decide if the world will fail him once more." Witness after witness described a childhood surrounded by drugs, promiscuity, and theft; a mother who was in jail; and a father who was a drug addict and dealer.

When Terrell was ten, witnesses recounted, he moved in with an aunt and uncle in West Virginia, but he longed to go back to his father in Pittsburgh, so they let him go. After his father died of AIDS, Terrell bounced from family member to family member, abusing drugs and looking for sex. Dr. Jolie Brams, a court-appointed psychologist from Columbus, testified that Terrell was born with an IQ deficiency as well as neurological problems. His emotional development was also deeply affected by being around people who abused and neglected him, despite professing their love.

Terrell also took the stand himself, in unsworn testimony, offering a perfunctory apology for his actions.

Despite the testimony from Terrell and his advocates, the following day, Wednesday, September 27, the jurors recommended that Yarbrough receive the death penalty, the punishment for which Stern had been pushing. Terrell muttered to the judge, "If I'm gonna die, then let me die." Bruzzese Jr. complied moments later, sentencing Yarbrough to death by electric chair for the kidnappings and murders of Brian and Aaron. He also sentenced Terrell to sixty-six and a half years in prison for the numerous other charges.

• • •

As they did at Nathan's trial, Rachel, Charlie, and Chris Muha, among others, offered their victim statements to the defendant. (The full version of Rachel's and Chris's victim statements can be found in Appendix A.) Again, the statements were filled with pleas that the convicted man own up to his guilt and open himself up to conversion. Rachel told Terrell:

> You can change and hope to go to Heaven, where everything is perfect, or you can stay the same and go to hell. In hell, you will be in pain all the time, forever. You will be in fear, forever. You will hate yourself and hate everyone else — and they will all hate you. Choose Heaven, Terrell.
>
> Terrell, you don't deserve any kindness — you didn't show Brian and Aaron any kindness. But Almighty God, who has the power and the right to take your life right now, is showing you mercy because you are His child, too. He is giving you time to change. But you never know how much time you will have. You could die tonight. Admit what you did and ask forgiveness. Then, start to make up for it, Terrell.

And, as she had done with Nathan, Rachel assured Terrell of her prayers for him.

Charlie Muha choked back tears as he stated: "I keep going over and over the sequence of events, how the burglary led to them being put in the car, to being shot. It'll never make sense. It's forever changed my life and the lives of my family."

When it was Chris's turn to speak, he underscored one point

the psychologist had brought up: that all of Terrell's life, people had told him one thing and then done another:

> But there is at least one person who has said one thing and actually gone through with it. And she has done this because she loves you and is so concerned about you. This woman is not a member of your family, it is not your co-counsel and it is not Dr. Brams. It is *my* mother. Even before you showed the police where the boys were, before she even knew you, she stood up in front of a packed church and chose to forgive you. And every day since then, she has fought back feelings of anger and rage. She has prayed for you every single day, so that you will change. *That*, Terrell, is love. That is a person who loves you [emphasis his own].

Following the trials, Terrell and Nathan were put in different prisons. When Rachel called the prison chaplains, she was told that victims are not allowed to contact those who have been convicted. Instead, it had to be the imprisoned who reached out. Rachel asked the chaplains to tell Terrell and Nathan that the family of Brian wanted to hear from them, to talk to them — and not to "beat them over the head." They had been forgiven. Both chaplains assured her they would pass on the message.

That was in September 2000. But the Muhas heard nothing from either young man. That is, until their second trials.

13
Back to Court

I have the strength for everything
through him who empowers me.

— Philippians 4:13

According to Ohio state law, when a defendant is sentenced to death, the case is automatically appealed directly to the Supreme Court of Ohio. As a matter of form, during the course of such an appeal, the court is permitted to review only the trial court record and not any additional evidence.

So when Terrell Yarbrough was sentenced to death by Judge Bruzzese on September 27, 2000, everyone involved knew there would be an automatic appeal. What they did not know, however, was that the appeal would result in a shocking turn of events that would drag the families back into court ten years after the initial crimes had taken place.

• • •

The question of jurisdiction had been debated soon after the bodies of Brian and Aaron were found. Because the crime had started in Ohio with robbery, burglary, and kidnapping, and then culminated in Pennsylvania with the double murders, the question had arisen about whether the cases should be tried in Jefferson County, Ohio, or Washington County, Pennsylvania. Jefferson County Prosecutor Stephen Stern stated shortly after the bodies were found that the trials could be held in either Pennsylvania or Ohio because the deaths were part of a burglary-robbery-kidnapping sequence that originated in Ohio. Stern had pushed hard to gain jurisdiction, saying in June 1999, "The citizens of Steubenville need to have this case presented here. It's … a crime that began in this community, took place here and ended here." Stern had also believed that common sense was on his side. "All Pennsylvania could prosecute is the homicide," Stern said. "We have the kidnapping, the burglary, and the robbery. Logically, you wouldn't want to try the case twice in two different places." But Washington County District Attorney John Pettit had been hesitant. "This is not a case which should go where someone wants it to go or thinks it should be," he said in the days after the boys had been found. "It should go where the best result will be obtained."

For two weeks, the debate continued among the prosecutors and in the media. On June 16, Pettit relented, stating at a news conference that he had decided not to file homicide charges against Terrell Yarbrough and Nathan Herring for the murders of Brian Muha and Aaron Land. Pettit said that after he and Pennsylvania state police reviewed the case together, they ultimately agreed that it would be best if juries in one state alone reviewed all of the evidence of all of the crimes committed by each defendant. He also said that having one trial for each defendant would be more compassionate for the families. "The issue here is not if I will give up jurisdiction to Ohio in this case," Pettit told the media. "The issue here is if Pennsylvania should arrest for homicide. We believe that, although crimes were committed to Mr. Land and Mr. Muha in Pennsylvania, the sanctity of their college and the city of Steubenville also were violated. That was not so in Pennsylvania."

This decision ended the debate on jurisdiction — or so all the parties thought. But the Supreme Court of Ohio, upon its review of Terrell's case, disagreed completely.

• • •

In a December 2004 decision, Chief Justice Thomas J. Moyer, writing for a unanimous court, said that because the murders of Brian and Aaron had taken place in Pennsylvania, it was that state, not Ohio, that had jurisdiction over criminal charges involving those deaths. As a result, the court overturned Terrell's convictions for aggravated murder, while sustaining the sentencing on the crimes of robbery, burglary, kidnapping, and other charges. Ironically, Pettit had told reporters in 1999 that it had taken him extra time to make his decision because he and Pennsylvania state police wanted to make sure that attorneys for the defendants would not be able to overturn any convictions in Ohio at a later date by making the argument that Pennsylvania should have had jurisdiction.

In the court's decision, Chief Justice Moyer took the judge and counsels involved with the first trials to task. "This is a regrettable case in which the attorneys involved — the prosecutor, defense counsel, and even the trial judge — failed to exercise the level of assiduity we expect of participants in the criminal prosecution of a capital case," he wrote. The chief justice added that there was no law prohibiting a retrial of the defendants for the murders in Pennsylvania. Moyer continued:

> The genesis of the error that mandates this reversal appears to be the prosecutor's failure to distinguish between the venue statute and the jurisdiction statute in drafting the indictment. Incorrectly relying on the language of the venue statute, both the state and the defense proceeded — indeed, through the appeal to this court — under the assumption that Ohio courts had subject-matter jurisdiction to try Yarbrough for aggravated murder when the homicides did not occur in Ohio, but in Pennsylvania. The Ohio jurisdiction statute, however — because of the limited manner in which the General Assembly has drafted it — simply does not provide jurisdiction over homicides that occur outside the borders of Ohio. See R.C. 2901.11.
>
> Nothing in the record reflects that the defense counsel or the trial court ever recognized this error — despite the fact that the prosecutor was seeking the death penalty. It was not until our review of the record and our request for supplemental briefing that the issue of the jurisdiction of the trial court over the aggravated-murder charges was addressed. See State v. Lomax, 96 Ohio St.3d 318, 2002-Ohio-4453, 774 N.E.2d 249, par. 17 (subject-matter jurisdiction cannot be waived and may be raised by this court, sua sponte, on appeal). One would expect that those charged with the responsibility of participating in the prosecution of a defendant who is subject to the ultimate penalty would exercise more diligence. In failing to observe the General As-

> sembly's statutory rules of jurisdiction, these attorneys disserved the citizens of Ohio and, in particular, the victims of these abhorrent crimes.

After hearing the supreme court's decision, Stern insisted that he had properly handled the original trials and accused the court of imposing an overly narrow interpretation of the statute of jurisdiction. "Now they're going to cost the state of Pennsylvania hundreds of thousands of dollars," he said. "Justice was not served here." Jefferson County Assistant Prosecutor Christopher Becker called the ruling "a great miscarriage of justice" and said he would ask the court to reconsider its decision. Nonetheless, the decision stood.

• • •

The families of Brian and Aaron were stunned. Four years had passed since the original trials, and they had thought their time in court was long behind them. Would they really have to endure another pair of trials? Chris Muha, who was by then in law school at Yale University, began seeking advice from law professors and other experts in the field, trying to find a way to argue against the Ohio Supreme Court's decision. But the supreme court had ruled.

Rachel, ever a woman of action, wanted to be sure that nothing like this would ever happen again to anyone else. She and Chris spoke with lawyers and contacts in the Ohio State Legislature and worked to introduce a new bill stipulating that if a crime starts in a state, then that state can prosecute it, no matter where it ends up. The bill, known as "Brian and Aaron's Law," was signed into law by Ohio Governor Bob Taft on April 12, 2005. But although the new law bore their names, it did not affect the Supreme Court of Ohio's ruling on the convictions for Brian and

Aaron's murders. Five agonizing years would pass between that ruling and Terrell's second trial.

At a news conference on Wednesday, February 8, 2006, John Pettit, the Washington County district attorney, declared that he would seek the death penalty against Terrell (who was serving his time in Ohio), and issued a warrant for his arrest for the murders. He said that he also planned to seek the death penalty for Nathan but wasn't ruling out a plea bargain option. Though Terrell was arraigned in Pennsylvania in December 2006 on charges of conspiracy and homicide, a series of delays — nine in total — pushed his second trial back until October 2009.

Most of the delays originated from defense lawyers seeking mental-health evaluations or other experts to evaluate Terrell's case. Retrying the case in Pennsylvania also meant a lot of pretrial litigation, Washington County Assistant District Attorney Michael Lucas told the media in October 2009; the litigation dealt with evidence and witnesses. And it didn't help that three different judges were assigned to the case as it dragged on. "It became a joke, because of it constantly, constantly, being pushed back," Rachel told the *Pittsburgh Post-Gazette* ahead of Terrell's Pennsylvania trial. "I think it's ridiculous."

The retrial for Terrell Yarbrough in Washington County, Pennsylvania, finally began on October 26, 2009; after eight days, a jury of nine women and three men had been selected. Common Pleas Court Judge John DiSalle sat on the bench. The prosecutor, Michael Lucas, presented his case to the jury much as had been done nine years earlier across state lines. "It was a nightmare because we went through every horrible detail," Rachel recalled years later. "The whole thing, from the beginning."

Kenneth Haber, Terrell's defense lawyer, however, said he would be presenting new evidence indicating that it was Nathan Herring, and not Terrell Yarbrough as previously determined, who actually committed the murders. According to Haber, two years after Nathan and Terrell were convicted in Ohio, a .44-caliber revolver was found in a heating duct in the home of Nathan's uncle in western Ohio. The gun was wrapped in towels. The search warrant was issued by police during the initial search of Nathan's home (the search that had turned up bullets and Brian's credit and ATM cards). The defense also argued that Terrell's life should be spared because he had led police to the bodies of Aaron and Brian and because he had been diagnosed as "mildly mentally retarded" many times since he was a teenager.

During his second trial, Terrell was highly emotional, Rachel recalled. Amid his tears, he would turn around and say, "I'm sorry. I'm so sorry." Nathan, on the other hand, was "like a stone wall" during his Pennsylvania court appearance the following summer, she remembered. "He was so hardened. And that was so heartbreaking."

On Tuesday, November 3, after six days of testimony from witnesses for the prosecution, mostly police and FBI scientists, Terrell was spared another tour on death row. Instead, after eight hours of deliberation, the jury convicted him of two counts of first-degree murder, and Judge DiSalle sentenced him to two life terms, along with an additional twenty to forty years in prison for conspiracy. Those sentences were to be carried out consecutively after Terrell finished his fifty-nine-year sentence in Ohio for robbery, burglary, and kidnapping. No determination was made on who actually pulled the trigger, but for Rachel, it didn't really matter, as neither young man had put a stop to the shootings either.

Terrell, for the first time in public, showed remorse for what he had done, and stated that he was a changed man. "I know an apology isn't even good enough," he said to the families shortly before his sentencing. "I just want you to know I didn't kill them."

The families encouraged Terrell to pray for God's forgiveness and to realize that, though he may not have pulled the trigger, he was just as much to blame for Brian and Aaron's deaths. "You were there and you could have prevented this from happening," Chris said. "Your life, though you don't deserve it, has value, and you can change."

"Terrell, we've been praying for you for ten years now and to see you stand up and say what you said is a good start," said Rachel at the conclusion of the 2009 trial. She continues today to hope for more. "If they would only say, 'I deserve what I got,' I would be right there lobbying to get them out," Rachel said in 2019. "I hope and pray that day comes. And I don't know, it could be tomorrow for all I know. Their hearts could be changing. But I don't know."

Terrell's was the only retrial that the families had to endure. On Thursday, July 8, 2010, Nathan Herring, whose murder conviction in Ohio had also been thrown out, pleaded guilty to the murders of Brian and Aaron and was sentenced to life in prison by Judge DiSalle. The Muhas were present, and Rachel again challenged him to change for the better in prison. For Chris's part, he shared with Nathan all the good done in Brian's memory since his death and the honor that God was bringing out of his brother's murder.

Rachel's brother, Rick, who was present at each court proceeding, said he had hoped that Rachel's and Chris's words and examples would help soften the hearts of Terrell and Nathan. "I was convinced that they were going to have a transformation, that they were going to realize that the people they affected do not have anger, do not have revenge, and have love for them," Rick said. "The second trials told them that. The second trials told them that this is a family that does not believe in revenge and does not want the death penalty for them."

Brian's uncle acknowledged that the outcome for which the family is praying may come in time, but it hasn't happened yet. No one in Rachel's family has had any contact from either man since 2010. Nathan and Terrell continue to serve their sentences in Ohio, after which they will be transferred to Pennsylvania to serve life sentences there. There is no chance of parole for them. In the meantime, the good work inspired by her faith in God and love of her son has kept Rachel going and has changed her life — and the lives of countless others — forever.

14
Working for Change, the Early Years

Do not be conquered by evil but conquer evil with good.

— Romans 12:21

Almost immediately after Brian's death, some members of the family approached Rachel and Chris and asked if they might like to start a charitable foundation in Brian's name. Rachel immediately agreed. The foundation's goal would be to raise money for scholarships: one to Franciscan University and another to St. Charles Preparatory School, both alma maters of Brian. The scholarships would help low-income young adults attend these schools and receive educations that might otherwise have been out of reach.

Thus, in the summer of 1999 was born the Brian Muha Memorial Foundation, Inc., a 503(c) nonprofit that would raise and distribute money for the good of society in Brian's name. The foundation was established in the spirit of Brian's own generous heart, recalling his 1998 decision to turn down the scholarship offered to him in favor of a student who needed it more. The foundation promotes and supports education through scholarship and tuition assistance and through distributions to specific organizations for related projects, programs, and activities. It also provides financial aid and assistance to relieve the plight of poor and underprivileged members of the community. The foundation's first officers were Chris Muha, president; Doug Ganim II (Rachel's second cousin), vice president; David Ganim (Rachel's cousin), vice president; Richard Ganim Jr. (Rachel's brother), treasurer; and Rachel Muha, secretary. Upon its inception, according to an early brochure, the goals of the Brian Muha Foundation were the following:

- To raise $350,000 for the Brian Muha/Aaron Land Scholarship at Franciscan University.
- To offer speakers to schools, churches, and other organizations with topics such as: How to forgive and why; Refusing to be conquered by evil; Brian's story: His beautiful life and beautiful death; Having fun and being ready for heaven at the same time; and How do we stop the killing? Brian's mission now.
- To establish summer and after-school programs for Steubenville-area young people.
- To establish Divine Mercy House at 165 McDowell, Steubenville, the house from which Brian and Aaron were kidnapped.
- To help revitalize off-campus housing, making it

safe for students and families.

- To offer financial assistance to Catholic schools in need.
- To increase the scholarship already established at St. Charles Preparatory School.
- To assist the recently established "Neighbors Who Care" organization in the LaBelle/off-campus area in Steubenville.

• • •

The foundation's first public fundraiser, the Brian Muha Memorial Golf Outing, took place on July 22, 2000, at Bent Tree Golf Club in Sunbury, Ohio, in conjunction with Rachel's family's reunion. It was the weekend of what would have been Brian's twentieth birthday. With expertise in fundraising, Doug Ganim II helped coordinate the event. Early on, Doug said, his motivation was to support Rachel in whatever way he could to try to help her heal. He wasn't much interested in the causes she was looking to support. "I just wanted her to have the support of her family," he said. But over time, Rachel's actions changed Doug's heart, as they have the hearts of so many others. "She taught us all about the lessons of forgiveness and love," including why suffering is allowed to happen and all the ways tragedies like the one they had experienced can bear fruit, he said.

The first golf outing cost $145 per person, and all proceeds went to the foundation. The effort raised $30,000 — a good start, but a far cry from the $350,000 they needed just for a scholarship to Franciscan University. Still, the foundation gave out its first scholarship just a year after Brian's death.

In a note written after that first fundraiser, thanking her family for their generosity, Rachel said:

> God forbid [any] more of us will die the way our Brian died — so how do we die triumphantly? Loving our enemies, praying and doing good to those who hate us, and giving of ourselves — always giving. If there is any truer measure of a human being than by what he does, it must be by what he gives. And you have given wholeheartedly, unselfishly, lovingly. We are so grateful to you — indebted forever. Every charitable act, you know, is a stepping-stone to heaven.

In order for the foundation to get donations, Rachel had to share her story often. She began by writing and speaking on social justice issues. In 2000, she gave eight talks on Brian's death and various subjects surrounding it. She addressed schools, women's groups, and religious and ecumenical gatherings, and she was able to speak in a personal, moving, thought-provoking, and motivating manner. Topics included Brian's story, forgiveness, how to refuse to be conquered by evil, the death penalty, how to end violence, and what will end the strife between Blacks and whites.

Rachel did not accept a speaker's fee, but she did accept donations of all sizes for the work of the foundation. Rachel describes herself as the "instrument" to tell Brian's story. "The Holy Spirit was palpable," she said, among those gathered at Franciscan during the four agonizing days of the search and the finding, and she determined that people needed to hear about it. Not that it was easy. Retelling Brian's story is always painful, and it is a sacrifice for her. The wound reopens each time. "It was hard, in the beginning, to get through speaking about it without crying," Rachel said in 2019. "Even today, it remains painful. But you know, we owe it to each other to tell the things we learn about God. We owe it, and I learned it not because I'm anything special, but because I had this terrible thing happen. So I owe it."

And Rachel sees and hears of the results of her efforts all

the time. "People come up to me and say, 'I haven't talked to my sister for thirty years, and I'm going to go home and I'm going to call her and I'm going to make up with her,'" Rachel said. People wonder: How can I not forgive the person who has hurt me when Rachel was able to forgive the ones who murdered her son? "I don't care if it's me telling it or somebody else telling it, but the story needs to be told of God's great goodness, and what forgiveness really is," Rachel said. In the year after Brian died, the donations that came in made possible a $12,000 gift to Christifideles School, a $25,000 fund for a scholarship to St. Charles, and over $9,000 to help defray the cost of the house from which Brian was taken.

• • •

However, even as the foundation's work was getting off the ground, Rachel found herself dissatisfied. Raising money for scholarships was good — but it felt more like a good start than the end game. She kept thinking about Brian's great love of children. As an older cousin, he had loved playing with the little ones at family gatherings. In Medjugorje at nine years old, he had bent down and talked to every child. Even before entering college, he had determined he wanted to be a pediatrician, to take care of children. "I remember Brian saying to me once when he told me he wanted to be a doctor: 'But I don't think I'm going to make a lot of money, and so probably nobody's going to want to marry me. But I don't care about making money, I just want to help the children,'" Rachel recalled. "And so all of that was in my mind."

And she kept thinking about the little ones who even now were growing up as Nathan and Terrell had. "They weren't born killers," she reminded herself. "They became killers. I was haunted with what happened to them."

Linda Ramsey, Rachel's close friend who had been with her every step of the journey, recalled Rachel's determination to help kids in need:

> She said to me, "I have got to do something to help stop this from happening and to help inner-city kids know about Our Lord and the difference between right and wrong and know that to hurt another human being is a terrible thing." Her main focus ever since Brian's death [has been]: What am I going to do to change things in the inner city, where kids don't have parents to help them? Her whole focus was she was going to take this horrible tragedy and make something good of it in Brian's name. And that's what she did.

Why, some might ask, would Rachel want to help people like those who took Brian? To her, at least in the beginning, that was the whole point. If children in the inner city were helped, maybe that would cut down on the number of lives that are senselessly taken away.

As the foundation continued its fundraising work through annual golf outings and she continued her speaking engagements, Rachel began making plans to help needy children directly and personally. She would gather together children from the inner city — maybe second- and third-grade students — once or twice a week for homework help. She would give them snacks and let them play games. She would teach them about God. She would bring them clothes. She would provide a safe, loving place for them for a few hours a week. Then, she thought, the kids would head home and be able to grow up well despite whatever situations they might find themselves in. Years later, she laughed at her naivete. "I knew nothing about what was really haunting inner-city people."

But that's where she began in 2005. As she was pondering a name for her new venture, the phrase "run the race" came to mind. She felt deep inside of her that this should be the name of her after-school program, but she didn't know why. "I thought, 'I don't even like to run, so I don't know why we're calling it that,'" she laughed.

One day, while reading Scripture, she finally understood. In the Letter to the Hebrews, it is written, "Let us rid ourselves of every burden and sin that clings to us and persevere in running the race that lies before us while keeping our eyes fixed on Jesus, the leader and perfecter of faith. For the sake of the joy that lay before him he endured the cross, despising its shame, and has taken his seat at the right of the throne of God" (12:1–2).

Relinquish every burden and sin. Keep your eyes fixed on Jesus. Run the race. Though she hadn't yet encountered these words of Scripture, they had been Rachel's interior focus ever since she had lost Brian. The Run the Race Club was born.

Part III

15
Let the Race Begin

Then children were brought to him that he might lay his hands on them and pray. The disciples rebuked them, but Jesus said, "Let the children come to me, and do not prevent them; for the kingdom of heaven belongs to such as these."

— *Matthew 19:13–14*

The first gathering of the Run the Race Club, held November 8, 2005, yielded one participant. Her name was Patty, she was eight years old, and Rachel surmised that the only reason she showed up at the basement of Holy Family Church in downtown Columbus was because her grandmother was a family friend.

The low turnout wasn't for want of advertising. Ahead of the event, Rachel and her friend JoAnn Markin had hung flyers in churches and schools all over Columbus's west side. When only Patty turned up, they realized that making and distributing posters might not be the most effective marketing strategy for their initiative.

But what seemed like a less-than-successful program launch was actually a hidden blessing. As Patty learned about the club — which started at twice a week for second and third graders — she almost immediately began suggesting changes. "She was telling us things like: You have to do it more often, you have to do it longer and have more age groups," Rachel recalled. Rachel listened to Patty's suggestions and, as time went on, started incorporating them. She also left the flyers behind and turned the recruitment of Racers fully over to God. "I thought, well, if God thinks this is something to do, then he'll spread it through the children," Rachel said. "Because it's always the children that he really loves."

The very next week, Patty brought some friends to the Run the Race Club. And then they brought their friends. And they brought their friends. Word of mouth was all that was needed, and Run the Race never advertised again. If the children love it, they'll tell their friends, Rachel learned.

• • •

Rachel had known since Brian's death that she wanted to be of service to children in the inner city — children who were growing up in the same challenging environment as those who had killed her son. While she first thought that work might be best carried out in Steubenville, it didn't take her long to focus on the problem in her own backyard.

Rachel set her sights on southwest Columbus — a part of town rampant with drug use, crime, gangs, and prostitution. Holy Family Church, with its rent-free basement in the crime-ridden Franklinton community, was an ideal place to begin. And Rachel's experience helping to run the Christifideles School when Chris and Brian were young provided her with a deep well of knowledge from which to draw as she envisioned her after-school program.

Rachel established the mission of the Run the Race Club, which was begun and sponsored by the Brian Muha Foundation, as follows: "To give love, friendship, guidance and support to young people, especially inner-city young people, so they can develop morally and intellectually, acquiring the virtues and attitudes needed for ever-lasting happiness." To achieve these goals, she began envisioning ways to support the spiritual, personal, and educational development of young people — all free of charge.

From its humble beginnings, the Run the Race Club, which in its various forms over the organization's lifetime is often called simply Run the Race, grew slowly but steadily. During the early weeks, Rachel and her team of volunteers planned club events around snacks, tutoring, and games. It expanded from two days a week to three and then to four. For the first six to eight months, about twenty Racers participated in Run the Race programs — the amount of kids that Rachel and JoAnn could transport in their vans. As Run the Race attracted more volunteers, the number of kids was able to grow.

But as time passed, Rachel and the volunteers learned that they really knew nothing about life in the inner city — or about the struggles with which kids there were dealing. Providing some food, clothes, and an hour's worth of fun was a start, but it didn't go far in addressing the real problems facing the young people who came. "We saw that the real poverty is emotional and spiritual poverty," Rachel said. "They don't know how to handle all the terrible things that happen, and they don't have God in their lives."

Rachel soon began to understand that the Run the Race Club experiment was going to be harder — and perhaps even more important — than she originally thought.

Over the next eight years, the club moved locations three times — first to a few rooms in a small office building behind Holy Family Church, then to the Holton Community Center on Eureka Avenue, and finally to its permanent location, on the corner of South Wayne Avenue and Eakin Road in Columbus's notorious Hilltop neighborhood, adjacent to Franklinton.

The permanent home for the Run the Race Club, known as the Center, is a 23,000 square foot, two-story brick building built in the 1960s as an elementary school for Columbus City Schools. When the city put it on the market in 2012, Rachel, who knew how important it was for the Run the Race Club to have a permanent location, believed it was the perfect fit. But though she had a generous benefactor who had offered to foot the bill, the asking price was an astronomical $750,000 — far too much to ask any one person to pay.

Taking the advice of her father, who had grown up during the Great Depression, Rachel offered Columbus City Schools $50,000. Much to her surprise and delight, the city accepted the offer, and the generous benefactor covered the complete cost. Acquiring the site was a huge win for the Run the Race Club, but having sat empty for more than a decade, the building was in terrible condition. The same benefactor who bought the building paid for its entire renovation, which came to approximately $750,000 and included a whole new interior.

"Everything you see, if you're standing in the Center, had to be repaired or replaced," Rachel said. "Absolutely everything." That included walls, floors, the heating and cooling system, the lighting, and the windows. The investment was worth it. Owning the building made all the difference in the world, Rachel knew, because it showed the club's permanent commitment to the neighborhood, and it offered area kids much-needed stability and security.

The Hilltop, where many of the Racers are from, is one of the most dangerous parts of Columbus. The majority of the population is white, with Blacks and Hispanics as the second and third largest populations represented. A report released in October 2021 by the National Network for Safe Communities at John Jay College said that seventeen gangs with an estimated 480 gang members were active in Columbus as a whole. Precinct 19, which encompasses the Hilltop, had the most homicides of any precinct in the city, the report said. Unemployment and crime in that part of the city — especially theft and burglary — both exceed the national average. And the area has the highest rate of fatal opioid-related overdoses in the city. By having a center of operations directly in that neighborhood, Rachel knew she could best serve those who most needed Run the Race.

• • •

Renovations to the new home of Run the Race were completed in May 2013, and the Center immediately became a hub of activity. Serving dozens of children ages five through eighteen, Mondays through Thursdays beginning at 2:30 p.m., the after-school club provided inner-city kids with food, games, help with schoolwork, field trips, clothing, and lots and lots of love. The majority of children coming to the Center, Rachel found, were second through eighth graders.

For many years, Rachel's philosophy was to keep the structure at the Center loose. The kids, faced with so many challenges in their lives, needed a place to run and be free — and even take some safe risks. She called it "freedom within boundaries." So the Center served as a place where kids could just be kids rather, than having to be tough on the streets.

The Center has nine classrooms — six upstairs and three downstairs — with additional spaces including a gym, a small chapel, and an office. An old boiler room was converted into a workshop. Each room is under the patronage of a particular saint, and a crucifix hangs in every room. Over time, these rooms have been used for music, as a salon, for art, and as a tumbling space. The chapel — with an altar made by a father and son for the son's Eagle Scout project — sits at the top of the stairs and serves as a safe, quiet space for Racers to find some peace when they need it.

Held at the Center, the Run the Race Club occasionally offered programs that taught trade skills such as plumbing, electrical, or woodworking for students beginning in middle school. There were places to play board games and sports, to be creative, and to run around outside. Every day, the Racers were fed a free meal, and a food pantry was available on site for those who needed a little extra assistance at home. Though the after-school program initially operated only on Mondays through Thursdays, other activities — like basketball, play practice, or dance and cheer team rehearsal — would often take place on Fridays and Saturdays.

"My goal was that anyone that came into Run the Race Center, wherever we were, felt a part of the family, and that they were loved and that they could depend on us," Rachel said. "They could come to us for all the Corporal Works of Mercy and the Spiritual Works of Mercy."

The Run the Race Club remained active during the summer months, providing alternative activities and events to keep kids off the streets and out of trouble. It offered sports teams, camps, games, and frequent trips to the Center's other property: Run the Race Farm in Galloway, Ohio, also sponsored by the Brian Muha Foundation. Teams from Run the Race have participated in all kinds of sports, from basketball to ultimate frisbee. A theater production company, Muha and Easley Productions, put on student-directed plays.

Every moment the young people can spend with Run the Race is valuable, and Rachel said she believes the "sweet spot" for being able to best influence the children is when they are in second to sixth grade. Once the kids enter area middle schools — which Rachel described as "war zones" — the transformation can be shocking. According to Rachel:

> The sixth graders go into middle school just as sweet as they were in the fifth grade, but by the end of the sixth, they're totally different. They're hard, and they're tough. They have to act tough and be tough. They have to have fought somebody somewhere along the line. They have to disrespect teachers. It's almost like if you don't do it, you're going to get picked on. Those are hard years for kids to begin with, sure, but then they have all this added pressure on them to be accepted.

Once the youths get to high school, they often spend less time at the Center because of jobs or sports. But it may also be for darker reasons: Maybe they've joined a gang or started selling drugs. "Miss Rachel," as she's called, never stops praying for her kids.

The programs operated by the Brian Muha Foundation are under the patronage of two saints: St. John Bosco, a patron of young people, and St. Martin de Porres, a patron of social justice. Born in 1815 in northern Italy, Bosco had a dream at nine years old that his life's mission was to be dedicated to the care and education of youth. Upon his ordination to the priesthood, he centered his ministry on bringing young people — especially the poor — to Christ. His words are on the wall of the Center: "If we practice charity, every community will be a little heaven." St. Martin de Porres, born in Lima, Peru, was the illegitimate son of a freed slave and a Spanish gentleman. Despite being ridiculed and despised for his heritage, de Porres dedicated himself to the service of others. He eventually became a Dominican friar and was gifted in his attentiveness to and care for the sick and those in need. The Racers learn about these saints and more at the Center, which offers children the opportunity to learn about the traditions of the Catholic Faith.

For many, many years, the primary focus of the Center was the Run the Race Club. Rachel estimates that at least five hundred young people have participated in the after-school program. In 2020, however, the COVID-19 pandemic struck and — as it did for the rest of the world — changed the way the Center would operate. That unexpected change set the Center's programs on a new course, turning a long-standing after-school program into a brand-new endeavor: a day school.

16

The Day School and the Farm

Do not conform yourselves to this age but be transformed by the renewal of your mind, that you may discern what is the will of God, what is good and pleasing and perfect.

— Romans 12:2

For years, the after-school program was the heart and soul of the Center. As time went on, though, Rachel found herself asking some serious questions: Are we doing the best we can to help people? Are we spending our time and our energy on the right things?

"We've learned so much over the years that the answer to

those questions is more and more becoming known," Rachel said in 2019. "You only have so much energy, and I want to put it to where it's used best."

While the after-school program, where Rachel gave the children freedom within boundaries, was fun for the kids, she noticed that kids needed dedicated help with their schoolwork, and saw that they weren't necessarily getting all they needed through the Run the Race Club. "The quality of education is so bad in the inner city," Rachel said. "We had them for three or four hours, and we weren't advancing their educational opportunities."

Over time, she realized that, while the kids greatly enjoyed the after-school program, it wasn't necessarily the best thing for them. "That was nagging at me," Rachel said. "OK, you're providing a fun place, and they're surrounded by people who love them. They're learning about God. But is their life going to be any better practically if we're not helping them educationally?" She began dreaming of a school — a place where Rachel and her team of volunteers could welcome fewer kids but for longer amounts of time. A place where they could provide young people with a solid, focused education in an intimate setting.

Then came the COVID-19 pandemic in March 2020, and the Center, along with the rest of the world, had to adjust. Suddenly, governmental restrictions were placed on gatherings, and the Center was forced to shut down for a time. Even after restrictions began to loosen, the number of kids who could be there at one time was still severely limited. So later that spring, Rachel made the tactical decision to move daily operations twenty minutes outside of town to the Run the Race Farm in Galloway, where, with more space, it was easier to comply with social distancing and capacity regulations. What was needed most, she determined, was a safe place where kids — so many of whom were now attending school remotely — could have the chance to focus on schoolwork during the day. With this change in location and operating hours continuing for the 2020–2021 school year, the Day School was born.

• • •

The eight-acre Run the Race Farm was purchased for the Brian Muha Foundation in 2012 by the same benefactor who purchased the school, and the first Run the Race Day was held there on May 31, 2012, the thirteenth anniversary of Brian's death. Though Rachel had planned for the event to take place on the anniversary, the Racers did not know the significance of the day. They played, ran, ate a lot of food, and enjoyed their first time in the country, Rachel recalled — though some of them found it to be too quiet. One reason the foundation bought the farm, Rachel said, was to give the kids a glimpse at life beyond the west side of Columbus — a glimpse they otherwise likely wouldn't get. Rachel knew that the young people needed a place to run around and to explore outside of the city that was, in many ways, so painful to them.

"Just driving from the inner city to the farm is a revelation to them," she said. "They say, 'Look at all this land' and 'Where are all the houses?' They just love it. They deserve that peace and beauty just like anybody else does."

Over the years, the farm became an important part of the Run the Race Club, and Rachel made a point to take the kids there once or twice a week — usually on Fridays — during the school year, and more often during the summer. The older Racers have helped to maintain it.

For the kids, the farm, located on a corner lot at 2500 Gardner Road in Galloway, is akin to Wonderland. About five of the eight acres are reserved for play and exploration, while two acres play host to a family of cows (at one time, there were also chickens, ducks, rabbits, goats, a pig, and a beehive on the premises). There's an outdoor basketball court and a trampoline and swings and a treehouse; there's a waterslide and little pool; there are climbing walls, a barn, and a big field. In the raised vegetable beds, Racers grow vegetables, both for their families and to sell at a local farmer's market. The farm also includes a farmhouse — a two-story, 2,700 square foot home with large windows and wooden floors — that has become a home away from home for so many kids. They frequently ask to spend the night, though Rachel always has to say no.

During the 2020–2021 school year, Bishop Robert Brennan, then head of the Catholic Diocese of Columbus, visited the farm for lunch one day to see the space and spend time with the kids. "When you go to the farm, you are met with a certain excitement and exuberance of children, and that's what's so beautiful about this," he said. "You know that these kids don't have much of a chance to be children, but when they're there, they're children and have all the regular joys and silliness of children. But it's all expressed in very healthy ways." Rachel allows the children freedom but also provides them with order and an environment that's rooted in faith, Bishop Brennan observed. "She tries to make that connection between faith and life habits, what they're learning about Jesus and what it means to be loved by Jesus," Bishop Brennan said.

• • •

With the start of the Day School, the after-school program was suspended. For the 2020–2021 school year, the Day School welcomed ten students to the farm for lessons and recreation from 9:00 a.m. to 2:30 p.m., all free of charge. Due to pandemic-related government mandates about gatherings and the school's limited number of volunteer teachers, they were only able to accept the first ten students whose parents called to sign up.

Because children, especially inner-city children, thrive in small environments, the small class sizes allowed them to breathe. Rachel and her volunteers used the Center's two vans to transport the young people to and from the farm.

The year of school at the farm was successful, so in September 2021, the Brian Muha Foundation officially launched the Day School at the Center. All the students involved in its first year wanted to return for a second, and Rachel wanted to welcome more students, so the school expanded to eighteen students for the 2021–2022 school year.

The transition to the Day School happened with fairly little drain on foundation resources. The Center already had the building and the desks, and an area Catholic school donated their used smartboards. Rachel had been worried about paying teachers, but it turned out that volunteers were at the ready. During the summer of 2021, volunteers and staff cleaned each room of the Center and adjusted the surroundings for school use. In many cases, the "fun rooms" with games and activities were combined with a more traditional classroom layout, offering a space for learning while still maintaining a space for playing.

The Day School operates similarly to a homeschool co-op, Rachel said, but instead of parents teaching kids, it's retired teachers, moms of older kids who have some time, and volunteers from the community. "They come in and they teach our little ones, and it's beautiful," she said. During this second year, the students ranged from age seven to age fourteen. With just a few students in each age group, they were able to get individualized attention and care from the teachers. In the 2021–2022 school year, the school day began at 9:00 a.m., and the students all ate breakfast and lunch together while they learned. When 2:30 p.m. arrived, marking the end of the school day, the children often asked to stay longer. "They're just a great group," Rachel said. "It's like a little family now for them."

In addition to the normal school subjects, Rachel hopes to teach the young ones at the school something less tangible: She wants them to learn what it means to love one's neighbor, and she wants them to learn compassion and generosity, even though so little has been shown to them.

The Foundation's programs receive many donations, so the kids are always on the receiving end of clothes, food, and other goods. Wanting to cultivate in them that care for others, Rachel decided to encourage the students to volunteer their time doing some yard work for people who were unable to care for their own homes. Somewhat to her surprise, the kids agreed, and Rachel found, through an organization in Columbus called Life Care Alliance, four families whose yards were in need of some attention.

"We broke the kids up into groups. They took rakes and shovels, and they went and cleaned up their yards," Rachel said. Upon returning to the Center, "one of the girls, without any prompting said, 'It is so much fun to help other people.'"

"I said, 'Thank you! That made it all worthwhile!'" Rachel said. "My point is that, yes, they're learning math and reading and all that, but they're learning so much more, and they love learning it."

The launch of the Day School at the Center brought with it a major shift: The after-school program, which had stopped due to COVID-19, began again, but in a much-reduced capacity. Rachel acknowledged the change. "That was our whole focus, after school," she said. "Throughout the years, we've tried many different things. And you just try what you think the community needs and what we're capable of doing. It has changed. We've learned so much about the inner city and the needs of the families."

The Center remains open after school a couple of days a

week for basketball or other sports, and it is also actively involved in producing plays, with all of the tryouts and rehearsals that entails. Over time, Rachel wants the afternoons to offer a "makerspace" where kids can focus on one extracurricular activity — be it art or woodworking or music — for a focused amount of time.

• • •

Rachel is still at the Center every weekday and sometimes on Saturdays. While the Day School is a lot of work, it is a commitment she finds worthwhile. With the arrival of the 2022–2023 school year, she hopes to expand even more. "I like that we're doing it kind of slowly because it eases everybody into it," she said with a laugh.

In addition to the volunteers, three full-time employees at the Center help keep things on track — and the beauty of these employees is that they are all former Racers, whose stories will be shared in a later chapter.

Wayne Anderson, twenty-two, handles all the gym and physical education classes for the students. He leads them in recess and introduces them to different sports, like volleyball and basketball. Daniel Houston, twenty-two, who loves to work with his hands, helps the children develop their woodworking skills. He has also taught reading and math. Cassie Seymore, twenty-four, who is studying for a degree in education, works with the fourth graders. "She just loves it. She set up her classroom and worked on it all summer," Rachel said. "It's remarkable to see this little girl who went through a pretty tough time find what she loves to do and is good at." Flex Barnes, nineteen, another grown-up Racer, works part time at the Center. "He can fix anything and everything and keeps the Center up and running," Rachel said.

Daniel and Wayne are also leading a "Young Gentlemen's

Club," and Cassie and Rachel a "Young Ladies Club," where they talk with the kids about what it means to be polite, respectful, and well-behaved members of society. For those unique programs, Rachel applied for and received a grant from the Catholic Foundation in Columbus — a nonprofit that, according to its website, "receives and manages assets to provide perpetual funding for the parishes, schools and ministries within the 23-county Diocese of Columbus." The grant will help Rachel bring in speakers and host events for the small groups.

As she looks toward the future, Rachel sees the Day School as the main focus for Run the Race. But regardless of what programs Run the Race provides, working with inner-city children will always mean there is more to learn — and constant challenges to be navigated. For the better part of two decades, Rachel Muha has worked to overcome the challenges facing the kids with whom she works — challenges that will forever remind her of those faced by the two young men who senselessly took the life of her son. Challenges that will forever spur her on.

17

Racing Challenges

The LORD is my shepherd;
there is nothing I lack.
In green pastures he makes me lie down;
to still waters he leads me;
he restores my soul.
He guides me along right paths
for the sake of his name.
Even though I walk through the valley
of the shadow of death,
I will fear no evil, for you are with me;
your rod and your staff comfort me.

— *Psalm 23:1–4*

If there was one thing Rachel knew from the start, it was that she wanted every single child affiliated with Run the Race to feel loved and that he or she belonged. She would frequently say that anyone who walks into the Center even one time was considered a Racer, and is automatically part of the family for life.

But there was something more that Rachel wanted, and it was that no one who walked through the doors of the Center would ever do any of the terrible things that Terrell and Nathan had done to Brian and Aaron. Rachel remained haunted by Brian's abduction and murder, and she was determined to help those who faced childhood challenges similar to Terrell and Nathan's in the hopes of preventing future senseless violence.

While she has been mostly successful in her quest, tragedies have still occurred. Some of the Racers have died, and a few are in prison for robberies or assault. One even committed a murder. "That just breaks my heart," Rachel said:

> He was eighteen years old, just like Terrell and Nathan. Grew up totally neglected. No father. Drug-addicted mother. Grandparents who were on and off helping him. He would come to the Center — not very often, but he would come — so I consider him part of our family. Always very quiet, never violent, never lost his temper. And then one night he broke into a house — just almost exactly like Terrell and Nathan. Except he knew the people he was breaking into. And he killed someone.

• • •

Because Rachel didn't have a real understanding of what the Racers were facing in their homes and in their neighborhoods when she started the Run the Race Club, she knew she had to learn and to listen. The more time she spent with the kids, talking to them and driving them home, the more she began to develop a better idea of what they faced on a day-to-day basis. And it wasn't pretty.

The streets in their neighborhoods were dirty and lined with broken sidewalks, and kids were walking around outside barefoot with no adult supervision. The kids would sometimes talk about how there was no food in the house, so Rachel would make a stop to get groceries on her way to the kids' houses. When she went inside, she found living conditions that were shocking. Mice, rats, and cockroaches run rampant in these homes. The kids often have bedbugs and lice. Because the yards are small and muddy, the kids play in the street, where cars line both sides.

"The first house I ever saw still gives me nightmares," Rachel recalled. "There were holes in the walls; there were cabinet doors hanging. In this particular house, there were six children — one in a Pack 'n Play. I learned later that the mother would give Benadryl to the baby to keep the baby quiet and sleeping, and that that is a common practice among inner-city moms — young moms who are overwhelmed."

Rachel recalls driving three small kids back to their neighborhood — a place she described as "in the worst section of the worst neighborhood" — and asking them why the family owned a dog. We have a dog and a cat, they responded. "Why?" Rachel asked again. "Well," the kids said, "the cat stays in the house to catch the mice. The dog stays outside to catch the rats."

In that particular family, the father lived in a different state, and the mother was addicted to crack cocaine. Those who are addicted to drugs often end up arrested and being separated from their children altogether. Rarely do they go into a drug rehab facility long enough to make any kind of a difference, Rachel explained. However, what does increase after rehab is the likelihood of a drug overdose, because their bodies can no longer withstand the same dosage they used to take.

Once, as Rachel was dropping a nine-year-old boy off at his house, he asked her if she would come for him tomorrow. She reminded him that, no, the Center was closed that day, and that she wouldn't see him until next week. "He got out of the car and before he closed the door, he said, 'Will you come anyway?'" Rachel recalled.

While some parents are supportive of the Center, others are not engaged with it, with some even wary of it. Rachel and the other volunteers walk a fine and challenging line when it comes to kids and their parents, for they teach the young ones to always be kind, respectful, and loving, even if their parents are engaging in inappropriate behaviors. Rachel recalled that one seventeen-year-old Racer described how angry he felt toward his father, whom he had seen only once in his life — angry enough, he said, to want to kill him.

"People don't know the pain they're causing to their own children," Rachel said, reflecting on that exchange. She tries to show the Racers that they have a choice in how they respond to the hurt, telling them that they're the ones who determine whether or not they will follow in their parents' footsteps and cause their own children pain in the future, or if they will decide to take a different path. "And they nod, but you just hope it works, [that] it sinks in," Rachel said.

Those trying to break that cycle of poverty, abuse, and drug use face tremendous odds. One longtime Racer, now in her mid-twenties, once called Rachel in desperation. She had two small children, but because of an abusive relationship with her boyfriend, she had been forced to move in with her mother, grandmother, and aunt — all of whom were on drugs. She knew she had to get her kids out of the house but had no idea where she would go. Rachel could only listen and agree that the young woman needed to get out of there. Rachel has hundreds of these anecdotes from her time at the Center. Everyone in the inner city, she said, has a story. "I learned that there's a whole world of problems — huge problems that seem overwhelming."

These anecdotes are backed up by facts and statistics. An October 2021 report released by the National Network for Safe Communities at John Jay College reviewed 107 homicides that took place in Columbus between January and September 2020, during the city's deadliest year on record. The report found that the crimes were most often motivated by money, drugs, and robbery. Many of those involved with the crimes — either suspects or victims — were young males between the ages of eighteen and twenty-nine.

Bishop Robert Brennan, who led the Catholic Diocese of Columbus from 2019 to 2021, reflected on the cycle of violence that continues within the city: "There are a couple of killings a week. And a lot of them involve either children or very, very young adults," he said in 2021. "It's a cycle because a culture of violence then creates a certain fear and a certain desire to be defended. And so then, the kids are getting guns, or they're looking for the protection of other people — but that's going to lead to more violence."

Bishop Brennan said he believes that one of the main causes of the violence among those in the inner city is "a poverty of hope" — the belief that, no matter what, things will never change. He continued:

> What Rachel gives and Run the Race gives is a different vision of life — that you're not trapped in that cycle of violence. And even though there are things going on around you, you're not limited to that. She gives the possibility of a different kind of life. And some of those children really take her up on it, and they're living very good lives right now. They've had experiences with education. Some of them are beginning now to raise their

> own families, but with stability. She shows them what's possible, and she also shows them that she believes in them.

• • •

Having a better understanding of the great challenges faced by the Racers and their families left Rachel with a decision to make. Should she try to address every problem she encounters, or should she continue to focus on the little ones? She decided to concentrate on the children, though she is always open to following the promptings of the Holy Spirit to serve those in need.

"That makes some decisions easier, some harder," Rachel said. "Being Catholic means being universal — it means the whole person, and so you want to address every need. You want to be faithful. But you have to choose, and that's why Saint Paul tells us we all have different gifts and we all have to work together."

When circumstances are really dire, Rachel has brought kids home, serving as power of attorney for them temporarily until the child's home life improved. For one, she became her legal guardian. "That's another sad thing," she said. "Parents who hardly know me are willing to sign over legal guardianship. I've often said what we really need is an orphanage — a residential home and school where we can take all the children in."

Hearkening back to Terrell Yarbrough's experience, Rachel spoke about how some parents don't want to give up custody of their children because they don't want to lose the governmental aid that they receive because of the little ones. Children in the inner city are facing a dearth of genuine love all around: from parents, from teachers, and from any other role models.

"In the inner city, you walk down the street and nobody talks to anybody," Rachel said. "Nobody looks at anybody. It's not a neighborhood. It's not even a community. It's just a place. There's such a breakdown of family and community and caring for each other. If that could be re-established, all the other things would fall into place."

Despite the challenges, Rachel never ceases to be amazed by the resilience and strength of the kids who come to the Center. She has also gained new insight into and appreciation for the innate human desire to enjoy life. "I often tell people when they come to the Center to volunteer, they see the children, and they're going to look like any other child that they've ever seen," Rachel said. "They're going to be running around playing, happy, eating, giggling, having a good time. But when you see the neighborhood that they came from, you can really appreciate the fact that they can laugh and have fun and want to."

Part of the job of Run the Race, Rachel said, is to help the kids learn how to have fun in a healthy way:

> I want them to enjoy life, and they want to enjoy life. The problem becomes when what they see is how they think you are supposed to enjoy life. When they see the pornography that their brothers and uncles are watching, or the videos that they have on constantly, or the drugs, or that fighting at the drop of a hat, or that getting drunk is the way to have fun. When they see all that, they think that's what everybody does. That's my fear. That's when they start to buy into it. That's when we start to lose some of them.

The hope that she can break this cycle is what keeps Rachel going. The journey has brought her beyond the after-school program and the Day School, extending the heart of the Brian Muha Foundation and Run the Race even farther into a community in need.

18
Beyond the Center

In every way I have shown you that by hard work of that sort we must help the weak, and keep in mind the words of the Lord Jesus who himself said, "It is more blessed to give than to receive."

— *Acts 20:35*

When the Brian Muha Foundation was established in 2000, the goal was to raise money to help underprivileged children attend two good private schools (St. Charles Preparatory and Franciscan University) in the hopes of offering them the chance at a better life. When Rachel wasn't satisfied with this more passive approach to caring for children in need, she started the Run the Race Club. In establishing a full-time school following years of providing an after-school haven for kids, Rachel found herself closer to her goal of being able to effect real change for children in the inner city. But those programs aren't all that the foundation has funded. Their work includes four other major initiatives as well: a land contract program, an immigration clinic, an online store, and holiday giveaways.

• • •

From its earliest years, the Run the Race Club began trying to find ways to improve the living conditions of its Racers. Many lived in run-down houses, and they often slept on the floor — sometimes on mattresses, sometimes not even that. To improve this situation, the Club started a Bedroom Makeover project where volunteers built beds for Racers who needed them, providing them with safe, sanitary places to sleep. It also began a Home Makeover project that devoted resources to fixing up the interiors and exteriors of Racers' homes that had fallen into severe disrepair.

A more comprehensive initiative unfolded when the Brian Muha Foundation began operating a land contract program in 2012. The foundation purchased homes in the Hilltop neighborhood, fixed them up, and then sold them to the families on the foundation's terms: what they determined to be at cost and with no interest. The mortgages ranged in length from ten to fifteen years, and families made payments directly to the foundation per contract. At the end of their contract, the families would receive the deed to their home.

The program, which Rachel sees as a key method of transforming impoverished neighborhoods, worked because a family's mortgage payment was able to be significantly less than their rent, especially as many lower-income communities in Columbus began to be gentrified. "All the people who lived there are trying to find a place to live that they can afford, which makes all the rents go up because there are more people," Rachel said. "It just turns my stomach because they have to pay $1,000 or $1,200 a month for a house in the inner city that's in a dangerous neighborhood, that isn't in good condition, and they have no choice. So they're trying to make these huge payments, and they're failing. They end up having to move or share."

Unfortunately, rising costs in real estate toward the end of the 2010s forced the land contract program to come to a halt; the foundation's most recent purchase of a house was in late 2019. "The price of houses has skyrocketed, so it doesn't make it worthwhile for a family," Rachel said. "Because even if we were to buy a house that should only be about $60,000 and is now $110,000, their monthly payments, in order to meet their obligation, even within twenty years — it's just too high for them," she said. "So I've had to say, as soon as prices come down — if they ever come down — or wages go up, or our income at the foundation goes up, we will continue. We just can't do it right now."

The eight families who had already purchased homes are doing well, however, and the long-term benefit is undeniable. "They've really been blessed — a $400 [monthly] payment on a house that we could rent for $1,000," Rachel said. "And they know that, and they're appreciative, and they're making their payments."

Owning a home means that families are more likely to take care of them, inside and out. And well-kept yards keep drug activity at bay. "When people are proud of where they live, that impacts the whole neighborhood," Rachel told *Woman's Day* in 2019. "It's a huge ripple effect. I wish we could buy 100 of these houses a year."

Cassie Seymore's family was one of the first to benefit from a land contract. "My dad just couldn't support the house, and we were getting evicted," she said. When Rachel bought a home nearby and was able to offer cheaper rent to the family, it offered them the long-term stability that they desperately needed. "That was the place that we stayed at the longest," Cassie said. "It was one that my dad was actually able to afford, even when work got slow. It was really helpful."

• • •

When Bishop Robert Brennan arrived in the Diocese of Columbus in 2019, he indicated that he would like to make caring for immigrants a priority and a focus during his tenure. The Brian Muha Foundation took note. As the immigrant population in Columbus grew significantly during the 2010s (the U.S. Census Bureau estimates that foreign-born persons made up 12.7 percent of the metro area's population as of 2019), the Center naturally started to welcome more children from immigrant families. These families, Rachel began to understand, needed more help than just food, clothing, or a safe place to play. They needed long-term security and stability without the threat of deportation hanging over their heads, and they needed trustworthy legal assistance.

Hoping to help provide a solution, the Brian Muha Foundation provided seed money in 2020 to launch an immigration clinic in Columbus through The Ohio State University's Moritz College of Law. The university had asked for a five-year commitment, but the foundation was only able to commit to one year. "It's a big chunk of money for us," said foundation president Chris Muha, himself now a lawyer in the Washington, DC, area. "We're going to see how it goes."

At the clinic, law students are learning how to become effective immigration lawyers, and the long-term hope is that the clinic will create a greater capacity for immigrant legal services in the state. The clinic is part of a long history of clinical legal education at Ohio State, and it offers students the opportunity to learn about immigration law practice, while assisting members of the immigrant community with their immigration cases.

"What happens in Immigration Court is that the Department of Homeland Security basically is pursuing individuals for removal from the United States," said Laura Barrera, visiting assistant clinical professor and founding director of the immigration clinic. "So it's a very high-stakes type of proceeding. You're usually looking at either being sent back to a place where your life is in danger, or potentially separated from your family and your community."

Unlike defendants in criminal court, where the stakes are also high, defendants in Immigration Court, though they have a right to an attorney, are not provided with one if they can't afford it. That means that immigrants are often left to represent themselves, while the government is represented by opposing counsel.

"If someone can't afford an attorney, then they'll just be by themselves, trying to fight their case," Barrera said. "Immigration law is notoriously very complicated. It's complicated even for lawyers. So people representing themselves in Immigration Court often don't have a very high chance of winning." When immigrants do have representation, however, their chances of winning their cases go up significantly. And that's where the Immigration Clinic comes in.

"As a clinic, we're focusing a lot on people who have these cases in Immigration Court," Barrera said. "I think that that right away provides a big and much-needed service, providing deportation defense services to people in our community that otherwise wouldn't be able to afford an attorney. That means it's much more likely that they'll be able to stay in the United States and stay with their families, or have a way to permanently live safely in the United States."

The clinic, which opened in fall 2021 and welcomes eight

law students per semester under Berrera's guidance, offers aspiring lawyers the opportunity to train with her in the practice of complex law, while providing a service to people in the community. Berrera is the attorney of record in the cases, and her students can represent the clients as student representatives under her supervision. The result is a win-win for the law students and the community.

"I've heard from the community how people are excited because of the need for the services we provide," Berrera said. "But then also there was a strong desire from the students to have more opportunities to learn about immigration law and immigration practice. So I've heard from a lot of people that they're excited about this new clinic."

• • •

In 2017, the Brian Muha Foundation purchased a storefront on Sullivant Avenue in southwest Columbus, just north of the Center. The idea was to create a place for selling discounted religious books and goods, and for kids from the Run the Race Club to sell things that they had made. In the bigger picture, the store would be a place where the Racers could learn basic business skills — like how to work with money, interact with clientele, and manage inventory.

Volunteers renovated the space, but just as its doors were set to open, the COVID-19 pandemic hit. For a time, they had to lock up the shop and leave it behind. The opening of the store was delayed even more when, on April 13, 2020, six young people broke into the space and vandalized it. They destroyed merchandise, lit T-shirts on fire, and sprayed fire extinguishers everywhere, causing thousands of dollars' worth of damage.

"We walked into the building, and it was just — I mean, all that hard work, and to see the young people that did the hard work with us, to see them devastated by people in their own community, was really the worst of it," Rachel said at the time in an interview with WBNS-TV, Columbus's CBS affiliate. To make things worse, the vandalism was streamed live on Facebook. "It was shocking to me to see these young people in a building, it's like somebody invading your home and destroying it on top of it," Rachel said. "I couldn't watch it all."

Continued problems at the storefront convinced Rachel to switch gears: Instead of having a physical store, they would move their business to an online store where they would sell T-shirts designed by the Racers. The foundation sold the building on Sullivant Avenue and launched a website. Currently, the Make It Happen Shop (brianmuhafoundation.org), as it is now called, sells a variety of shirts with faith-filled designs and text.

Cassie Seymore, one of the Center's full-time employees, oversees the store, which is now connected with the Day School. Students from the school are given the opportunity to get to know every part of the business. "Not only are they learning how to make T-shirts, they're learning how to design, how to make profit, and the business side of it," Cassie said. The T-shirts are created using a process where designs are printed onto sublimation paper and then transferred to the T-shirts using ink and heat with a special printer. The shirts can be made on demand as orders come in through the online store.

Income from sales, Cassie said, goes back into the business to purchase more supplies or pay the workers for their time and effort. The Racers love seeing their designs come to life, she said, especially the art lovers among the older girls. "It really brightens them up. It makes them excited and want to learn," Cassie said. "Knowing that actual people are placing orders for them, it really makes them excited."

• • •

The Foundation also works hard to connect willing donors with families who need a little extra support during the holidays. For Easter, it offers a free ham or a gift card for families in need, provided by donors. The foundation also provides all the side dishes, prepared and donated every year by Catholic students from Bishop Ready High School nearby. On Thanksgiving, families are offered a free turkey or a gift card. For Christmas, the foundation runs a family adoption program where families are connected directly with donors so that donors will have a good sense of what each particular family needs.

In terms of gifts, the foundation used to get Christmas lists from the kids, Rachel said, but over time they realized that those needs were being fulfilled by other organizations. "But then I thought, what about things like a little crèche, or a beautiful Christmas ornament?" she said. "So now we give things that the kids wouldn't normally get."

• • •

Other foundation initiatives, like a preschool for the youngest children, have come and gone over the years. The change in priorities and focus exemplifies a foundation that is nimble and constantly seeking to meet the needs of an ever-changing community.

Rachel could not do the work alone, nor does she. At her side are her champions: the Racers she has served over the years, and the volunteers, donors, friends, and organizations who have her back.

19
Racer Champions

Do you not know that the runners in the stadium all run in the race, but only one wins the prize? Run so as to win.

— 1 Corinthians 9:24

It is impossible to look back at everything Rachel Muha has accomplished over the past two decades and not be astonished. Of course, she would be the first to say that she has merely been the figurehead for the work God wanted to accomplish through her and Brian. Nonetheless, even God's plans take a willing collaborator — just look at the fiat of the Blessed Virgin Mary, whose powerful words in response to what she learned from the archangel Gabriel, "May it be done to me according to your word" (Lk 1:38), changed the course of human history.

But Rachel could not have accomplished all that she has without the little ones to whom she is devoted, and who have placed their trust in her and the Run the Race Club. And of course, Rachel could not have accomplished all that she has without plenty of coworkers in the Lord's vineyard who have volunteered their time, talent, and treasure to help her and the Center over the years. They — the youths and the volunteers who serve them — are her champions.

Only in recent years has the Center been able to support full-time workers. And those workers are also the Center's primary success stories — three Racers who attended when they were young and now are giving back to the next generation of kids in need. These kids-turned-employees know firsthand the many challenges facing the families on the Hilltop — challenges that the Run the Race Club, and now the Day School, are trying desperately to mitigate.

• • •

Cassie Seymore has been part of the Run the Race family since she was seven years old — back when the Run the Race Club was still located at Holy Family Church. Brought to the Club by neighbors, Cassie discovered the family atmosphere that was missing in her own home life.

At home, she faced promiscuity, poverty, and abuse; Run the Race was her safe haven. "I was there all the time," Cassie recalled, adding that she took "any escape that I could get from home to be able to eat or to just be a kid." At fifteen, when she couldn't take things at home anymore, Cassie ran away. Rachel was eventually able to adopt her, and Cassie went to live in Westerville with the mother figure who had, all of a sudden, become an actual mother. It was this transition, even more than her time at the Center, that changed Cassie's life. "If I would have stayed living with my dad, I probably wouldn't be involved at all," she said. "I'd probably be going down a path I don't necessarily want to."

Now twenty-four years old, Cassie is working full time at the Center while studying part time to get her college degree in education. She focuses her attention on the Day School and the online T-shirt business. "We're doing a ton of things at once," she said, "but it's great."

And she really feels like she can be an agent of change for the next generation of kids coming to the Center. "I really try to influence them when they're here," Cassie said. She shares with them her story of overcoming her own serious struggles in an effort to help them stay motivated to make good choices. "The Center is not just a center," Cassie said. "It is another home outside of home. You're surrounded by people who genuinely care and respect you, and just want the best for you. That's what you're really going to get here versus any other youth group where you go and play. It's a lot greater than that."

• • •

Daniel Houston, twenty-two, is another Racer champion who is now employed at the Center full time. At first, he didn't want to come to the after-school program, but finally did so at thirteen at the urging of a family friend.

"I remember Miss Rachel met us, and she's like, 'Come on in, are y'all hungry?'" Daniel said. "So we came in, we ate, and then we just started coming every single day after school and even on the weekends. We tried to ask her, 'Can you open up on the weekends?'" He also began bringing his friends.

"If Miss Rachel is hearing this: I love you, man. I appreciate everything you've done for me," Daniel said, smiling. "She's just been supportive, you can talk to her about anything. She's smart, she's very caring. She's like the grandma, the auntie — she's like the mom. She's got open arms, for real. She don't care what you look like, how you act, she just wants the best for people."

Without the Center, "I think my whole life would have been different 'cause pretty much since that day I've been coming here," he said. "I don't know what I would have been doing, for real. Like I really don't know." Growing up, Daniel faced poverty and violence. He knows how hard it is not to be influenced by certain people or drawn in by certain temptations. "You really gotta think about your life," he said. "That just kept my mind straight."

Now, it's up to him to be the welcoming face that Rachel was to him to the next generation of Racers. He teaches woodworking to the students at the Day School, and he spent the 2020–2021 school year at the farm teaching fifth and sixth graders. He hopes, first and foremost, that the kids who come to the Center are able to have fun. "A lot of kids, they grow up too fast," he said. I went through that when I was a kid. So just always try to have fun." Daniel also hopes they take advantage of all the opportunities that the Center has for them, and that they learn how to be good kids and make good choices in their lives.

Daniel has seen the great effect the Center has had on the community in general. "Her impact on this neighborhood has been big," he said. "She's just always trying to do what is best for people. We don't got a lot of people that's out here doing stuff like that." Watching Rachel help the kids at the Center, Daniel has learned how to help people. "Being with her these last ten years basically helped me see people," he said. Now, Daniel said, he wants to become involved in social work so that he can continue to do similar kinds of work.

• • •

When sixteen-year-old Wayne Anderson began going to the

Center, he was a self-professed hothead. "I would get into fights and try to fight people," he said. But "the more they worked with me, the more I came to the Center, and my attitude started changing and changing. It made me the person who I am now."

The person he is today is a twenty-two-year-old full-time employee of the Center who serves as both gym teacher for the Day School and general janitor. He organizes games and sports for the students, like volleyball, football, and relay races, and he loves the time he gets to spend with them. "I love being around the kids," he said. "We have fun, we laugh. Nobody['s] perfect, so little stuff happens, but I love the kids."

Though many of the kids who attend the Center were born and raised on the Hilltop, Wayne isn't quite sure where he is from. His family moved around so much when he was growing up that he never had a proper home. That is no longer the case. "The Center is a good place. It's like a home where we can just be free," he said. "You can just make friends, run around, eat, have fun, and be yourself."

• • •

There are too many young people positively affected by the programs of the Brian Muha Foundation to include by name, but two other Racer champions are representative of the hundreds who have come through the doors over the years. Charles "Travon" Easley, a lifelong resident of the Hilltop, was brought to the Center by a family friend when he was just five years old. Now he's seventeen, and his life has been molded in part by Rachel and the Center. "One thing about Rachel: She can bring people back," he said.

At Rachel's encouragement and insistence, Travon attended Columbus's Catholic Bishop Ready High School. After graduating in 2022, he enrolled at Capital University in Columbus. "I made it very far with her help and her guidance and her love," he said. "I definitely feel that not only has she made an impact on me, but she's made an impact on my family. She's made an impact on this community." Travon is not sure how his life would have been without the Center and without Rachel, but he does know that the Run the Race Club has "brought a lot of light to my heart." He continued, "I always knew she was going to be there."

When Travon was in a production at a city theater camp, Rachel organized a group of Racers to attend the final performance. Someone in the theater company asked him, "Who are those people?" "That's my family," he responded.

When Travon wanted to start a theater company as part of the Run the Race Club, Rachel was completely supportive: Muha and Easley Productions was launched, and the Center has hosted several plays. "The Center opens doors for everybody, not just me," Travon said, adding that he hopes that he will leave the kids with a love of the arts when it's time for him to depart.

DeShay Mills, seventeen, raised in Columbus, first started coming to the Center in 2015, when she was in fifth grade. It was summer, and Rachel was throwing a big party outside. Because DeShay enjoyed herself, she started attending the Run the Race Club's regular activities. Her home life was bad, and she didn't want to be there. "There was a lot of stuff going on in my family and too much going on in my life. So I just wanted to do something. And then I just kept on coming back, coming back, and Rachel really lifted everyone up — always making people happy and stuff if you're down. So I really enjoyed that."

When DeShay was younger, she liked hanging out with everyone, meeting new people, and helping with the new kids that arrived. Now, she sees herself in the younger kids who, like her, come to the Center looking to escape struggles at home. "It feels good," she said. "I get to talk to them. Help them out. See what they're struggling on. Talk to them if they're having a bad day or something." In short, she tries to be a little bit like Rachel.

• • •

For these champions, Rachel has provided not only a safe and fun place to spend time but also a new way to look at life. She is raising a new generation of kids and modeling for them the way of love. "She doesn't play favorites. She doesn't have go-tos," Travon said. "If you're a Racer, you're a Racer. That's just the way she brought us up."

And her example has made an impact. "If you see a kid walking, you give them a ride," Travon said. "If you see a kid with his pants hanging down, you don't ask him why. Instead, you give him a meal and take him home. Why? Because that's what she's done for us," he said.

Clearly, through the Run the Race Club, a new cycle has begun to replace the old one: a cycle of kids looking out for kids, a cycle of generosity and care for others, a cycle of unconditional love — no matter who you are or what your story is.

20

Supporter Champions

Since we have gifts that differ according to the grace given to us, let us exercise them: if prophecy, in proportion to the faith; if ministry, in ministering; if one is a teacher, in teaching; if one exhorts, in exhortation; if one contributes, in generosity; if one is over others, with diligence; if one does acts of mercy, with cheerfulness.

— *Romans 12:6–8*

Outside of the three full-time employees, the Center runs completely on volunteers. Rachel has never taken a salary, though she works upwards of seventy hours a week. Now, with teachers needed on a regular basis for the Day School, volunteers are even more critical.

"Consistency is so important," Rachel said in an interview with *Woman's Day* in 2019. "We say to these kids, 'We're here, no matter what.' That's the real work of Run the Race. The donated clothes, sports equipment, and school supplies bring the kids to the Center. But what keeps them here is that they know we love them."

Over the years, at least 250 volunteers have donated more than 130,000 hours of their time and talent in support of the Center and the Run the Race Club. Some have taught a class or a special skill. Others have organized events, like the annual Night of Champions fundraiser that supports the Brian Muha Foundation. Still others have simply spent time with the young ones, offering their attention, care, and support. Countless individuals and organizations have donated money, food, clothing, or other needed items. "I see us as a sort of hub," Rachel said. "We're this place where people who want to help can come and help, and the people who need the help get the benefit of their help."

• • •

When longtime Run the Race volunteer Nancy Drought moved to Columbus in the early 2000s, she heard about Brian's murder and thought how terrible it was. A few years later, she heard Rachel give a talk on forgiveness. "It was so powerful, her message, so deeply poignant — to forgive someone who had murdered her child. I thought to myself, 'I don't know if I can do that,'" Nancy recalled. Rachel's witness of forgiveness made such an impression on her that Nancy knew that "whatever she had going on, I should be a part of it."

Nancy began volunteering for Run the Race before it settled into its permanent location. Depending on her own kids' stages of life, she helped with different degrees of volunteering over the years, including teaching art to kids who were kicked out — or who failed out — of school, and assisting with the Ready, Set, Race Preschool when it was in operation.

"You get attached to the kids, and you just want the best for them." Nancy continued:

> But I think it's most important just to show up, just to be present, because that's where trust comes in. When you show up, you let them know this is a warm, safe place. Then, if anyone were to open up and need some help in other places of their life, they feel that they could do that here. But it takes time, and it takes people to show up.

Andrew Winkel, a friend of Brian's from St. Charles and now a foundation board member, helped out at the Center in the early years. Hearing the kids' stories, he couldn't help thinking of Terrell and Nathan and how they had grown up. Yet "feet away, here's Rachel, not thinking of herself, but thinking about [the kids in need]," Andrew said. "She would just give her time and resources and then try to bring other people into that fold. It was amazing." At her side, he became even more aware of the importance of patience and understanding.

"One of the things Rachel's shown is that if [the kids are] showing up, they want help," he said. "They need help. They want to be there. This is really important." Like Nancy, Andrew recognizes the importance of presence — just being there for the kids. "You need to be present," he said. "You need to be giving them your attention, helping them with whatever it is they need, whether it's schoolwork, whether it's just talking, or whether they want to play basketball."

• • •

The Run the Race Club has also been lifted up over the years by hundreds of supporters of all different stripes. It has been the recipient of countless behind-the-scenes monetary donations and untold gifts for the kids. "Not everyone can be here physically," Rachel said, acknowledging that different people give in different ways. When the Center or a family needs something, all Rachel has to do is ask — and sometimes she doesn't even have to do that. "I can send an email out and say our food pantry is empty, and people fill it up and fill up extra rooms of food," Rachel said. "That's amazing to me. I am in the presence of so many good people."

Rachel's brother, Rick Ganim, who has been on the board of the Brian Muha Foundation since its inception, believes the success of Run the Race is due to two specific things: Rachel's "wonderful leadership qualities," and the fact that so many people over the years have gravitated toward her story. As a result, they have contributed generously to the work she is doing. Her son Chris added that Rachel's authenticity is what makes so many people willing to partner with her in the work of the foundation. "She knows what she's doing and why she's doing it," he said.

Donations range from the organization-changing kind, such as the money to purchase the Center and the farm, to much more targeted, local efforts. An organization called the Friends of the Foundation, started by Rachel's neighbor Jetta Wright, consists of a group of twenty women who raise funds every year for coats, pajamas, food, and more for the Racers. The Run the Race Support Club at St. Francis de Sales High School in northern Columbus elects student officers and plans events for the Racers each year. "The Racers love being with them year after year, even when the faces change because the high schoolers graduate," Rachel said.

In addition, Upper Arlington's chapter of Rotary International has helped cut down trees and chop wood on the farm. Parish religious education classes have hosted bake sales. Rachel frequently comes home to donations on her front porch — everything from bikes to food to household items and more. Groups also give of their talents; for example, in 2015, the Columbus Folk Music Society, a group of musicians who have a passion for sharing their art, started an after-school music program at the Center.

Gifts come from all over, including from one couple who heard of Run the Race early on and sent Rachel a box of crucifixes. Grateful, yet unsure what to do with them, Rachel stored them away. After the Center was purchased, she found there were just enough for one crucifix to go in every room of the building.

• • •

For years, members of the local chapter of the Christ Child Society have donated ingredients, labor, and time nearly every day to make and deliver home-cooked meals for kids at the Center. When Run the Race Club moved to the Center, the society also provided money for tables, supplies, and closets for the art room.

Barbara Groner, the president of the board of directors of the Christ Child Society of Columbus and also a board member of the Brian Muha Foundation, said that she was hooked from the first time she had heard Rachel's story in 2009. At the time, her son had recently graduated from St. Charles Preparatory School, Brian's alma mater, and was getting ready to leave for college. "You think about how every parent's worst nightmare is to send your child to college and something horrific like this happens and they don't come home, you don't ever see them again," Barbara said. "So if the least that we could do to help Rachel in her quest to save some of these inner-city children is to bring home-cooked meals, like absolutely, sign me up."

As of 2021, the Christ Child Society has nine Run the Race meal teams comprising more than sixty volunteers. Their involvement grew from feeding kids at the Center twice a week during the after-school program to providing two meals a day — breakfast and lunch — for the Day School when it was at the farm during the pandemic. Starting in fall 2021, the organization began providing breakfast and lunch at the Center almost every single day, and in early 2022, when the Center restarted after-school activities on Wednesdays only, the society began covering dinners on those days for the kids. They also provide summer snack bags and host holiday parties at Thanksgiving, Christmas, and Easter.

"Our mission at Christ Child is helping children in poverty. Our motto is 'Nothing is ever too much to do for a child,'" Barbara said.

> Food insecurity is so real, and just life insecurity is so real for so many [more] inner-city and at-risk children [than] we realize, and Rachel has told us many times, that sometimes it is just the lure of a home-cooked meal that gets some of these kids in the door at the Center and keeps them off the street and gives them a safe place to go. So we feel that that really connects with our mission for children, and that it really is a fantastic partnership.

"Sometimes I hear people will be like, 'Well, can't she get government assistance or government meals?' and I thought, 'You're kind of missing the point,'" Barbara added. "It is that message of: You're worth it. You're worth having a good meal. It's worth preparing for you. It's that message of love and concern and care for these kids. That's the beauty of what we do."

Rachel knows that she could not do what she does without the support of so many. "I'm so appreciative of all the volunteers, the people who give their hearts and souls and don't have the reason behind it that I do," she said. "You know, when somebody just drives down to the Center and gives their afternoon to be with these high-energy kids — that's amazing to me. And I'm so grateful for all the volunteers, people who give us donations who could be giving their donation somewhere else, and they see some value here."

• • •

All champions — Racers and supporters — are honored at the annual fall fundraising gala for the Brian Muha Foundation. This "Night of Champions" has taken the place of the golf outing as the primary fundraising event for the foundation, and the monetary goal is generally around $200,000 — though that goal is often exceeded. Held in the stunning Walter Commons at St. Charles, the event includes talks, entertainment, a sit-down meal, a silent auction, and a live auction.

The first Night of Champions took place in 2016, having evolved from a fundraising luncheon at Villa Milano, a banquet and conference center in Westerville. The largest event so far took place in 2019, pre-pandemic, when five hundred supporters came together for the good cause.

Jaime Winkel, wife of Andrew, who has helped run the event for the past several years, works with a committee of ten other women to organize the dinner, seek out donations for the silent auction, and recruit new attendees. "There's a conscious effort on spreading the word as much as we can to new supporters each year," Jaime said. Items donated to the silent auction range from the large (a week's getaway at a Montana vacation home) to the small (a variety of themed gift baskets with plenty of goodies). One of the big-ticket items is a meal that Rachel helps to prepare for ten to twelve people at someone's home; she then shares with the group the story of Brian and the foundation.

The school-age Racers do not attend the event, but older

or former Racers often attend to share their stories or provide entertainment. Jaime and her team build the event website, and then share it through the foundation's network to encourage donations to the auctions. "We spend a good six months before the event contacting people and asking them to donate to the auction," she said.

Jaime hopes that people who attend the Night of Champions leave feeling both a desire to support the foundation and a desire to share what they have learned with others. The event is "about sharing Brian's story, and it's about sharing information on the Center and the organization and the mission," Jaime said, "but it's also about celebrating so many champions that exist in this space that we're in. It truly is a night of champions."

Bishop Robert Brennan attended the Night of Champions both times it was an in-person event during his tenure in Columbus. He called it "very moving," noting that "it is more than a fundraising event, it really is a telling of the story, and it's just very, very inspiring." The bishop was also inspired by the *way* Rachel shares her story. "There's nothing in it where she's trying to put credit on herself or what she does," he said. "She acknowledges what she had to do by way of forgiveness, but really she's always shining the light on other people. So she tells the story of what happened to Brian, and how it devastated her, and the long-term effects of it — but the real gist of the story is her belief in the children that she is serving."

It is love of those children that motivates Rachel to continue to share her story and invite others to be a part of it (see Appendix B for the text of her talk at the 2021 Night of Champions). And as with every other part of her life, she simply chooses to have faith. "We have to raise the money for the foundation to be able to give money to the Center, so we're going to always be raising money," Rachel said. "But isn't that always the case? It'll come. It always has."

21
The Role of Faith

We know that all things work for good for those who love God, who are called according to his purpose.

— Romans 8:28

In Jerusalem with his disciples, as related toward the end of the Gospel according to St. Matthew, Jesus shared a series of parables, stories that he frequently employed to illustrate spiritual or moral points, with his followers. Just before his arrest, suffering, and crucifixion, Jesus shared one of his most important lessons, clearly stating what Christians are called to do in this life if they want to attain eternal life in heaven:

When the Son of Man comes in his glory, and all the

> angels with him, he will sit upon his glorious throne, and all the nations will be assembled before him. And he will separate them one from another, as a shepherd separates the sheep from the goats. He will place the sheep on his right and the goats on his left. Then the king will say to those on his right, "Come, you who are blessed by my Father. Inherit the kingdom prepared for you from the foundation of the world. For I was hungry and you gave me food, I was thirsty and you gave me drink, a stranger and you welcomed me, naked and you clothed me, ill and you cared for me, in prison and you visited me." Then the righteous will answer him and say, "Lord, when did we see you hungry and feed you, or thirsty and give you drink? When did we see you a stranger and welcome you, or naked and clothe you? When did we see you ill or in prison, and visit you?" And the king will say to them in reply, "Amen, I say to you, whatever you did for one of these least brothers of mine, you did for me."
>
> Then he will say to those on his left, "Depart from me, you accursed, into the eternal fire prepared for the devil and his angels. For I was hungry and you gave me no food, I was thirsty and you gave me no drink, a stranger and you gave me no welcome, naked and you gave me no clothing, ill and in prison, and you did not care for me." Then they will answer and say, "Lord, when did we see you hungry or thirsty or a stranger or naked or ill or in prison, and not minister to your needs?" He will answer them, "Amen, I say to you, what you did not do for one of these least ones, you did not do for me." And these will go off to eternal punishment, but the righteous to eternal life. (Matthew 25:31–46)

With this story, Jesus indicated that we are judged according to how we live the heart of the Christian life, what he called the greatest commandments: to "love the Lord, your God, with all your heart, with all your soul, and with all your mind" and to "love your neighbor as yourself" (Mt 22:37, 39). This is what Rachel Muha has done in abundance, and her Catholic Faith serves as the foundation for it all.

"If you ever want an example of somebody who brings light into darkness, that would be Rachel," Bishop Robert Brennan said. "She's motivated by faith, she brings forgiveness, and she brings belief. She believes in changing the lives of other people so that [the cycle of violence] doesn't repeat itself."

At the same time, while Rachel's faith and desire to bring good out of Brian's death were her primary motivations for beginning her work in the inner city, those motivations expanded over time. "It wasn't just helping the poor because our Church tells us to help the poor," she said. "It became helping the poor because that is what they need. It wasn't centered on me or Brian. It was transferred and was centered on them. And that's what really brought joy."

• • •

By media and friends alike, Rachel has been called a "living saint" and an "everyday hero." She has been compared to Mother Teresa. But she scoffs at all of that. Instead, Rachel simply does what Jesus asks of us all, and she gives God all the credit. "People ask me: 'How do you do it?'" she said shortly before the twentieth anniversary of Brian's death. "I say, 'I'm not really doing it.' I mean, I might be the person you see, but if I didn't have God giving me the grace and the strength I need, I could not do it, because it's hard. It's the hardest work I've ever done. But it's the most joyful work I've ever done, even in the midst of these terrible sufferings that the children have to survive."

She considers sharing God with those who come to the Center to be the most important part of her work. It's significant that crucifixes are all over the building, there is a designated chapel, and each room has a patron saint. Rachel knows how much the children she serves don't know about God — and how much they would benefit from an encounter with him. She said:

> I look at the children and I think: "Almost none of them have been baptized. Almost none of them have received confirmation. Most of them have never been in a church. And yet they're happy. They can laugh. They're optimistic." When you ask them, "What do you want to be?" they want to be scientists and doctors. If they can be that without the sacraments, imagine what they could be with the sacraments. I think we who receive the sacraments, we take them for granted. And we don't realize the power they give us, and what they could give the kids.

It is for this reason that Rachel makes it a point to teach the children who come to the Center about God — telling them Bible stories and stories about the saints, and hoping and praying that they will ask for more. The children also write letters to God, helping them develop a connection with him that Rachel said was beautiful to see.

> They need God — we all need God in our lives — so I just want to give that to them as much as we can. Inner-city children especially need the strength and the grace and the power of God because they're facing so many obstacles. I really do think that one reason why there are so many struggles in the inner city is because a lot of people don't have God in their lives. I want the

> children so much to know how much they're loved by him and that they can turn to him and he hears them. He'll answer the way he thinks he should answer, the way he knows is best for them, whether they know it or not, but he is there. And he loves them.

Rachel frequently takes the kids from the Day School (and from the Run the Race Club before that) on field trips to different Catholic churches in Columbus. Someone from the parish will meet them there, show them around, and explain the different aspects of the sanctuary. "They're just amazed at the beauty of a church," Rachel said. Then they'll go out for ice cream. "They love that," she added, with a laugh. "They think that's the greatest thing ever."

She also regularly takes the kids to Eucharistic adoration — the practice of worshiping Jesus in the Blessed Sacrament outside of Mass. The children love it, Rachel said, and it has even led to some conversions. Over the years, twelve Racers have been baptized, and some have gone on to receive first Communion and confirmation.

"With Miss Rachel, you learn about God, but not only do you learn about God, but it strengthens your faith," said Travon Easley, seventeen, who converted to Catholicism as a twelve-year-old. "I'll never forget when I first came (to the Center) — yeah, I believed in God. But by the time I kind of departed, I had a new love for God." Travon recalled: "Miss Rachel took me to church all of the time and would ask: 'What questions do you have?' and, 'Do you understand why this is so beautiful?'"

This type of growth in relationship with Christ is "exactly what we pray for" for the young people, Rachel said.

Rachel also makes it a point to speak with the kids about the dignity of the human person. Back when she was involved with Columbus Right to Life, she didn't imagine that she would one day be proclaiming a pro-life culture to inner-city kids. But when she found that an abortion mentality runs rampant in the community she was trying to serve — particularly among the older students — Rachel was grateful for that background.

"The little ones, pre–middle school, are extremely pro-life and in total disbelief that our country allows abortion," Rachel said. "But then they're just surrounded by the mentality that you go on birth control when you're fourteen, and if it fails, you get an abortion. Literally, they say, 'What's the big deal?' So to undo that abortion mentality is real."

• • •

In reflecting on the role that the Catholic Faith has played in Rachel's work, Bishop Brennan said that faith isn't just about putting on a pair of rose-colored glasses and saying that things aren't as bad as they look. Instead, "faith — and Rachel really lives this — faith is really acknowledging the evil that exists but looking deeper into reality to see the hand of God, to see what God might be asking us to do or what God might be asking me to do in this moment," he said. "She certainly has that faith in the eternal and in life with God forever. She's very motivated by the fact that she will see Brian again, and she'll be reunited with him and with God."

Bishop Brennan also believes that Rachel's faith comes across not only in what she does, but in how she communicates Brian's story and her work, despite still missing her son greatly. "She talks about the loss, and she says, 'I will feel that every single day.' But she's not looking for pity," Bishop Brennan said. "Part of faith is acknowledging that evil — not just evil that happened twenty years ago — but acknowledging the evil that she feels even now. That sense of loss is as painful today as it was ever before. So to me, that's real faith. That's not just illusion — that's not just dampening down the pain. It's seeking that deeper meaning and letting that faith inspire her to great actions."

After every interaction with Rachel, said Fr. Mick Kelly, the family friend who was a student at Franciscan University when Brian was killed, one is left with a feeling of peace and joy — even if she happens to be correcting you. She seems to know intuitively how to handle each person that she meets, he said, and she has a way of being able to gently persuade people to do what needs to be done.

"There's a different kind of deep strength that comes from Rachel Muha that isn't easy to describe because it can only be encountered," Father Kelly said, who added that she has about her a "sense of the holy." "There's no question of disobeying her," he said. "There's no thought. It's not possible. As soon as that woman asks for something, you're going to give it to her, out of a tremendous and deep and profound respect that is holy."

"She has the ability to command men twice her size and half her age like I've never seen before," he added, laughing. "It's incredible. I don't know how she does it." Father Kelly has heard it said that when someone would stand in the presence of Pope John Paul II or Mother Teresa of Calcutta, he or she would feel like the only person in the world, with "all the love of the world focused on you." He believes that's the effect Rachel has on others, too.

In many ways, Bishop Brennan said, Rachel's work is the "perfect example" of what Pope Francis means when he asks Catholics to be more attentive to those on the edges of society — the cast off, the forgotten, the poor, the marginalized. "You don't just open up a center and say we'll wait for everybody to come to us," Bishop Brennan said. "You go out into the peripheries. She went right into the neighborhood. She goes to find people to bring them along."

"There's so much that's fake in the world and in the world

of religion — claims made by people about what's Christian and what's not," Father Kelly said. "It makes me angry sometimes, because I saw it. I saw the reality of what it is to be a Christian. And I saw somebody live it nearly perfectly."

22
Much Fruit

"Amen, amen, I say to you, unless a grain of wheat falls to the ground and dies, it remains just a grain of wheat; but if it dies, it produces much fruit."

— *John 12:24*

When Brian Muha was shot and killed on May 31, 1999, his life was cut tragically short. At eighteen years old, he had his future before him. College graduation, a satisfying career, perhaps marriage and a family. Family reunions and laughing with friends. Prayer. Travel. Hard work. Lots of Lebanese food. He had nothing but time, until he had no time at all.

In a perfect world, Brian would have lived a full and happy life on earth. But ours is not a perfect world. When sin slithered into the Garden of Eden, evil infiltrated humanity — the same evil that would one day cause faces to be battered and bullets to be fired, shattering countless hearts in an instant.

No hearts were more broken than those of Charlie, Rachel, and Chris Muha.

The murders of Brian and Aaron were terrible. They were brutal and senseless. They launched an exhausting search and a tri-state media circus. They brought about trials and retrials. They inflicted untold amounts of pain and deep, lasting sorrow and longing.

But his death is not what Brian Muha will be remembered for. Brian's spirit lives on today, stronger than ever, in the lives touched by the work done in his name and in his memory. Why? Because his mother has seen to that. This petite, stubborn, determined, delightful, faithful woman of God was not going to let a beating and a bullet deprive the world of the joy and the good she knew her son would have brought to it — and was already bringing to it. But she could only make that choice because of her intentional and steadfast decision to rely on, trust in, and cooperate with the God she loved and needed so much, come what may.

Rachel's faith and work mean that Brian lives still. Jesus' teaching that the grain of wheat that dies produces much fruit (see Jn 12:24) is borne out in the legacy of the eighteen-year-old from Westerville, Ohio. Acting as God's instrument on earth, Rachel has, in the wake of tragedy, harvested the fruit of God's Holy Spirit: "love, joy, peace, patience, kindness, generosity, faithfulness, gentleness, self-control" (Gal 5:22–23) — all characteristics Brian manifested in his life.

• • •

This fruit of the Holy Spirit has been made manifest in Rachel's decision to forgive her son's killers, and in the impact her decision has had on others. "I don't know how many of us in that position would take that path," said Barbara Groner of the Christ Child Society. "I think we hope we would, but how difficult is that? And how beautiful is it that she's able to do it."

Fr. Mick Kelly said he didn't understand what forgiveness really meant until he witnessed it being lived out. "I didn't understand what it is to know, 'Father, forgive them for they know not what they do.' I didn't understand the 'Our Father': 'Forgive us our trespasses as we forgive those who trespass against us.' I didn't understand any of that," he said. "I was a twenty-two-year-old man, and I had no idea. Because I hadn't seen it yet. Then I saw it."

"Even to this day when people get mad about things, I always say, you know what, if my sister could forgive those boys that killed my nephew, I'm not going to be upset about this — whatever the thing is," Debbie Callihan said.

The Spirit's fruit has been made manifest in the faithfulness of a woman who purposefully used her son's death as a way to live her faith and to pass it on to others. As her son's killers awaited trial, Rachel counseled and catechized family and friends about heaven, forgiveness, justice, and mercy. "Remember, the God who created us without our cooperation will not save us without it," she wrote in a letter in 2000. "We must cooperate. We must do God's will. We must use trials and sufferings of our lives to become holier."

The Spirit's fruit has been made manifest through the many prayers that have been offered for Nathan Herring and Terrell Yarbrough for two decades. "I would be so happy if they would realize that they've had advocates — me and Chris and members of [our] family and friends for all these twenty years — that have been praying for them and hoping that they would make their time in prison their path to heaven," Rachel said. "I want them to have every chance possible to make up for what they did on earth so they could go to heaven."

The Spirit's fruit, shared by Rachel, has been made manifest in the lives of the young people of inner-city Columbus whom she has loved as her own, caring for them and introducing them to God. "I've never met a woman like her in my whole life," said Cassie Seymore. "Being able to take something that tragically happened and still wanting to help the same type of children in the same type of community must have really been hard. It's beautiful seeing that she would want to prevent more children from turning out like Terrell and Nathan."

Brian would have been proud watching his mother work with children as he had wanted to, Cassie said. "She is helping the children spiritually, mentally, physically, and not only is she helping them, but they're helping her too," she said. "It's beautiful to see and to be able to be a part of it and grow with it." "I love what she's doing," said Wayne Anderson. "Ain't nobody out here trying to do what she's doing, trying to get kids off the street. I know it's not going to happen overnight, but she's working on it, and you don't see nobody else doing that." Travon Easley added, "Not only is Miss Rachel always there, but she is continuously always doing something for someone."

The Spirit's fruit has been made manifest in the joyful admiration of her remaining son. His mother, Chris said, is genuine, loving, and tenacious. She's dedicated and tough. She works long days on her feet and never stops pushing to make things better. "It's been truly amazing and at the same time sort of like — that's what she does," Chris said. "It's amazing but not surprising." Their mother's work in Brian's name is "just like a lesson — a testament to concrete acts of love, done one day at a time, seeing where they take you," Chris added.

The Spirit's fruit has been made manifest in the lives of Rachel's friends, who are in awe of her example and strive to emulate it. It is because of Rachel's example that family friends Dave and Linda Ramsey made the decision to welcome their great-nephew into their home so that he could escape a bad situation in his own home life. "I thought, my gosh, if she can do it, I'm going to do it, and I'm going to get this boy out of this mess," Linda said. "She is the most selfless person I have ever met. She puts everyone and everything above herself. She has changed my life and my family's life."

With small children of his own, Andrew Winkel often finds himself wondering how he, too, can be more like Rachel, and how he can help others in some small way. He also desires to pass that example on to his own children. "Seeing it in action is powerful," he said. "I want them to see what happens at Run the Race and why it's important to help other people."

Father Kelly said that Rachel's example has enhanced his vocation to the priesthood. "Rachel gave me a vision for someone who is absolutely free," he said. "Rachel gave me a vision for somebody who is kind and loving. Rachel forgave some terrible boys who were leading terrible lives, not because they deserve that forgiveness or had any claim to righteousness, but because they were just like Brian. They both became the son she lost." With Brian's murder, a good young man died, but his death is not the end of the story, Father Kelly observed. Nor is vengeance, nor even justice. "Brian's legacy is the legacy of mercy. Of taking pity, of suffering for your fellow man."

Barbara Groner said that Rachel is inspiring simply to be around. "She's just such a kind person and she just reminds you all the time to just be kind and be forgiving," she said. "I feel like she doesn't sleep. Her mind and her heart are always trying to find new and different ways to reach another child — another opportunity. What she does is infectious."

• • •

While the programs of the Brian Muha Foundation have accomplished much over the years, Rachel still feels that there is more to be done:

> We have given away tons of clothes and food and furniture. We pick up furniture now and deliver it. We've given away cars, and we've helped with jobs. But I still don't feel we've done enough as far as changing hearts. I want all the Racers to have that relationship with God, and that's not happening fast enough for me. So I don't feel that we've accomplished that goal, and I don't know that we ever will. People try to tell me that you're planting seeds and all that. I know that, but I want to see those seeds grow. So I never feel like we've done what we set out to do. There's always more.

What's she proud of? "That's a hard one," Rachel responds. "I don't think I'm proud of anything," said the woman who has devoted her life to serving others. "I don't think I'd say I'm proud of anything." But she does have some advice for anyone listening.

First, there is nothing that people can't get through as long as they have God on their side. "I want to give that hope — the promise of God that he is here and he will protect you," Rachel said. "Yes, it will be hard. No, it doesn't take away the pain. But he gets you through and brings you to the other side where your memories are sweeter because they're not tainted with any anger or revenge."

Second, don't spend time worrying about the future, because you never know what might happen. "Spend your time in communion with God, and then whatever happens in the future, you can get through it with God," she said.

Third, never be outdone in generosity. "After Brian's death, I came to realize that giving everything is really the goal and the joy of being a Christian, and that we can never get there," Rachel said:

> No matter how much we give, and God loves that, there's always more to give of ourselves. There's always more of our way of thinking, or way of being, or way of teaching, or way of dealing with people: There's always a refinement going on in our souls. I've come to really love that. I love that you can never stop giving of yourself. You can never stop sacrificing, you can never stop offering, you can never stop being, hopefully, better and better. The Christian life is not stagnant. You never reach a threshold that you can't go above. You can never say, "Now I know what I need to know, and now I'm a Christian, so there!" And that's so exciting. What could be better than to live your life knowing that tomorrow I could be a little bit closer to God than I was today, and I could give him even more?

Rachel Muha has lived a remarkable life, and she has done so freely and in the service of love. In doing so, she has ensured that her son, whose life ended far too soon, lives on in the hearts of everyone she encounters. And it is her prayer that those she meets strive to embody the characteristics of the one she lost.

"Be compassionate. Put yourself aside. And love children," said the mother of Brian, Chris, and so many, many more. "They're everything to God."

Brian in Fátima, Portugal, Summer of 1997

Run the Racers with the blankets they made for their families as Christmas gifts.

Run the Racers and volunteers at The Run the Race Center.

Columbus police officer and K9 officer visit the students at The Day School.

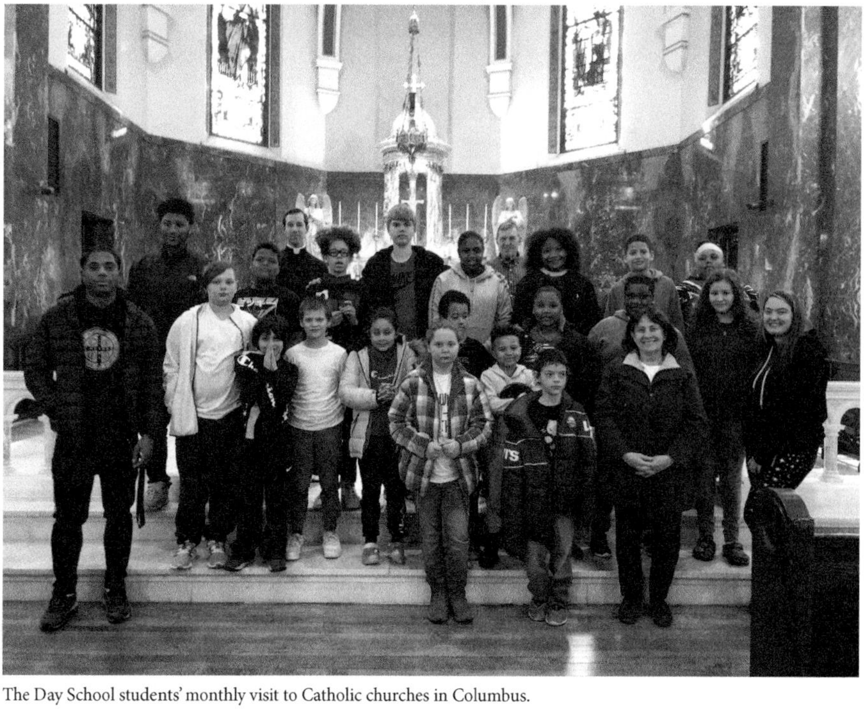

The Day School students' monthly visit to Catholic churches in Columbus.

Afterword by Rachel Muha

My sheep hear my voice; I know them, and they follow me. I give them eternal life, and they shall never perish. No one can take them out of my hand.

— *John 10:27–28*

I like to think of Brian hearing the voice of his Savior right at the moment of his death. Maybe he heard Jesus calling him, and he immediately followed. And Jesus proves that "no one can take them out of My hand."

It's a comfort. But it's also a heartbreaking image: Brian, showing the marks of his Calvary, following Jesus Christ, bearing the marks of the Calvary. Both walking toward heaven, Brian following his Savior. Both taking on a new countenance as they get farther away from earth. A beautiful countenance. Brian becomes more and more at peace, happier and joyful to the point of almost bursting because he knows this will be forever.

At first an intense loneliness overcomes me. I want to go with them. Yet I can't. All I can do is watch. Watch the distance grow. Feel the longing grow. I want to run after them. "Wait for me! Please wait for me … Brian …"

He can't.

As I long for him, I realize I want him to do exactly what he is doing. Following Our Lord to his Father's house. And so I am at peace. I realize and am happy that Brian's life and mission on earth is not over. The way he can accomplish his mission has changed, but his mission has not ended. Nor will ours end when we aren't on this earth anymore. Isn't that a sweet thought? It is what the Church has always taught. There is the communion of saints and we all belong to it. We take on our work while we are here on earth and, please God, when we go to heaven. All together. How beautiful.

So as I pray that I will hear these words, I also pray that Brian heard them — hears them still: "Well done, good and faithful one. You have run the race and now you're home."

I love you, Brian.

— Mom

Acknowledgments

I am deeply thankful for the many people who helped make running this written race possible. I am especially grateful to Rachel Muha and her son Chris for being open to sharing such a painful part of their past with me and for trusting me to tell their story.

I am grateful to Debbie Callihan for keeping such detailed and exceptional notes and information from the time of Brian's death and throughout the trials, and for sharing that information with me.

A heartfelt thank you goes to all the many individuals who openly spoke to me about Brian's death and the aftermath — conversations that even twenty years later naturally remain very difficult.

Thank you, also, to the editors at OSV who helped prepare this manuscript, especially Mary Beth Giltner, who entrusted me with the job of bringing Rachel's remarkable story to life.

I am deeply thankful for my mother, Eileen Crowe, who read and edited the manuscript, and on whose impeccable literary judgment I rely immensely. Thanks, too, to my father, Michael Crowe, and my in-laws, Robert and Debbie Heinlein, for their generous care of my family when I was writing.

When it comes to my immediate family, my gratitude knows no bounds. My children, Joseph, Anne, and John, were generous with their patience as Mama worked, and they prayed with me every night for Rachel Muha and her ministry. My husband, Michael Heinlein, was my first and best editor. He cared for the kids when I was busy writing, chauffeured me on trips to and from Columbus, and was my unfailing cheerleader. Without his support, this book would not have been possible.

Finally, I am most grateful to our loving, merciful, and forgiving God, whose story this ultimately is. To him be the glory, now and forever.

APPENDIX A

Full Trial Victim Statements of Chris Muha and Rachel Muha to Nathan Herring and Terrell Yarbrough (2000)

The following statements were made to Nathan Herring on August 30, 2000, in Jefferson County, Ohio, court during the penalty phase of his homicide trial.

CHRIS MUHA TO NATHAN HERRING

Yesterday, Nathan, you took that stand and you led us to believe that you're sorry for what you've done. You know what? I don't believe you.

Yesterday you took that stand and made it appear as though you were crying. And you know what? I don't believe you.

Yesterday you took that stand and you told us how much you loved your brother Ricky and how much his death devastated you. And you know what? I believe you. I believe you because I know exactly how strong the love is that exists between brothers, and I know exactly how much it hurts when a brother is gone.

We've heard a lot about you and Ricky. Well, let me tell you a little about me and Brian. Brian and I were only a year apart and because … of that, we did just about everything together when we were growing up. We had the same friends. We played at the end of the street together. We would go exploring down the creek behind the neighbor's house. We rode our bikes everywhere, played Nintendo for hours. We traded baseball cards. We went to school, grade school, for six years. We went on to high school together. We got even closer then. We even had a class together because Brian was so smart. We served in student government together where he and I were president and vice president of the school. Every decision made by the student government came down to us, and together we realized how much responsibility we had, and we grew so close in that.

We talked about ways to make our school better, things we could do to help others out. Helping people out was one of Brian's greatest traits. He always had time for somebody else.

We heard a lot about your athletic potential and how it all seemed to vanish with your leg injury in eighth grade. Brian went out for football for the first time his freshman year and he would have done outstanding, but you see, Nathan, up until eighth grade Brian had a bone problem in both of his heels and ankles. His bones were rubbing together so painfully that at times he couldn't walk or run, but he never complained. He never used his injury as an excuse when he tried out for football.

He never complained that he had lost years of experience to the other kids. He never complained that he wasn't as good as he could have been because of his injury, and he didn't need the excuses either. By the end of his sophomore year he was starting varsity. The next year he played offense as well and, in fact, the two of us together were the starting running backs. Muha and Muha, everybody would say. I was number five and so he chose number six.

I used to love driving home with Brian after our football games. We would talk about the game in the Blazer about what we did good, where we messed up. We would laugh and think about what we could do better, and I was thrilled when Brian decided to follow me to Steubenville. I knew it was a choice he didn't want to make at first, but he did end up making it, and we really grew closer there. We again played football together, and we ended up winning the flag football championship because Brian scored all 20 points in the final game.

We would have breakfast together at 7:30 a.m. because he wouldn't get up for his class. So I had to call him to wake him up.

But I think the part I liked the most was driving home in the Blazer with him for breaks because it was just the two of us and we could really talk about things that we couldn't talk about otherwise. Those were real special moments to me, and driving home alone is one of the hardest things that I do now.

Yesterday you took that stand and you told us that you had a bad feeling before you went to that track meet. You told us that you thought something was going to be wrong. And you know what? I believe that, too. I believe it because I had the same thing. In fact, I had two.

The first one came a few weeks before you killed my brother. I had a dream, and when I woke up, I had it in my mind that I was supposed to prepare myself for something that was going to cause me incredible suffering, more than anything I had ever gone through. I thought it was odd, and I didn't know exactly what it referred to, but I began to pray for strength.

The second one came three weeks later. On the Friday before May 31, Brian asked me if I could be home on Monday morning, the morning of the thirty-first. That was going to be the first day he was gone. He said that he was going to have flowers sent to my mom that morning and wanted to make sure I was there to get them in case she wasn't. When we got the flowers at about nine thirty that morning, I read the note which said, "Just wanted to say hi even though I'm away. Love, Brian." When I read it, I had a strange feeling as though Brian was gone for a really long time. "That's kind of weird, I thought to myself. He's only going to be gone for a month." I shook it off. I certainly didn't connect it with the dream I had three weeks earlier, at least not until Detective Lelless called about five hours later telling us that Brian was missing and that there was blood in the house.

Was this the incredible suffering that I was supposed to be preparing for? Was Brian really gone for more than just a month? I wanted to believe so much that he was alive, that he was hurt somewhere and that I would find him. I pictured myself brushing aside a pile of leaves and finding my brother lying there bleeding and hurt but still alive. I dreamt of carrying him to safety and rushing him to the hospital where he would eventually get better. I hoped so much that that was what the incredible suffering was going to be, not what it actually turned out to be.

Nathan, don't you wish that you could have been there to save Ricky? Imagine if you had been there. I mean, imagine if you had jumped in the water and pulled him out. Imagine how great you would feel. That's the expectation and the desire that I had for five days, five days of searching while you knew exactly what had happened and exactly where he was, and as we both know, that hope of mine was never fulfilled. As we both know, Brian was dead even before those flowers arrived. He truly was away, as he had said in his note. The incredible suffering was indeed his death, and not just his death but his brutal beating and murder.

It is because of you that this has happened. It is because of you that I have lost my brother, that I am going through what you went through. You have admitted to being responsible for the murder of my brother. I will hardly be able to think of Brian without thinking of you. You have become forever associated with him for me. I cannot help but see him when I see you, think of him when I think of you. Whether I like it or not, you are one of the closest links I now have to my brother. You were the last person to see him alive. In a very real way, my memory of my brother will always be attached to you.

My brother and your brother are gone. God willing, they are both in heaven. God willing, they are brothers now. All that remains is for you and I to become brothers. You cannot turn back the hands of time like you said but you can do the next best thing. You can become like my brother was, and this is something only you can do because only you have this connection with him.

But you are nothing like my brother, but you can be, but only when you are truly sorry and not just for what happened but for what you have done and for what you have become, and that will only happen when you are willing to accept your punishment, not because you have no other choice now but because it is what you deserve for killing my brother.

I have been praying for you every day since May 31st, and I want so much to believe that you are sorry, but until you willingly accept your punishment and try to become the person my brother was, you disgrace the memory of your own brother, and I cannot believe until then that you are sorry for taking mine. It's only by becoming good that you can turn back the hands of time and give me back my brother, as much as that is possible.

RACHEL MUHA TO NATHAN HERRING

Nathan, I am grateful to God and happy to say I am Brian's mother. I gave birth to him. I held him when he was born and looked at his face and couldn't believe how good God is to give me a second son, a son any mother would be proud to have.

I love my son, Nathan, and I want to tell you about him, but first I want to tell you a story. It's a story about a beautiful young girl named Maria, and it's a true story. She lived on a farm in Italy years ago and a young man named Alessandro worked on the farm and saw how beautiful Maria was, and he wanted her. She was not only beautiful on the outside, she was good on the inside, and so she knew that if he had his way, he would not only go to prison but he could go to hell forever. So she avoided him.

But one day he grabbed her and he threw her on the ground and he held a knife over her and she still fought him, and so his passion turned to anger, and he stabbed her fourteen times, and all that rage left him, and he got scared, and he ran away, and he left her there to die a slow death, and before she died she forgave Alessandro.

Alessandro was caught and put in a county prison, just like you. He was only eighteen years old, just like you when you killed Brian and Aaron. He went on trial and was proud and scornful in court. He denied up and down that he had anything to do with killing this beautiful girl. He pretended he was being treated unfairly and acted amazed that anyone would think such a thing of him, but the evidence was overwhelming.

They brought in a psychologist, just like your lawyers did. That didn't work. So they blamed his troubles on the fact that his mother died when he was young and his father was an alcoholic. They said that when he was around twelve he started hanging around with bad kids who taught him bad things and used bad language, just like you. He didn't go to church anymore. He turned his back on God and his face to the devil, just like you, Nathan.

He was found guilty and at that time an eighteen-year-old was still considered a minor. So he was given what they call the light sentence, and the light sentence at that time was thirty years hard labor. He worked hard all day long and slept with the rats and the roaches at night.

He was sorry, Nathan. He was sorry for getting caught and sorry that he had to spend so many years in prison, but he was not sorry that Maria's life was taken from her, just sorry that his life was going to be so awful. Is that just like you? For his first eight years in prison, Alessandro stayed hateful and mean and proud, and then one night Maria appeared to him in his cell and he was terrified, and he called the guards and he told them that he saw her more beautiful than she was on earth because now she was in heaven. You see, Maria had been praying for Alessandro from heaven.

The next day he admitted that he killed Maria, and he asked God and her family to forgive him. He stayed in prison until his thirty years were up, and he came back to town a changed man. He wanted to repair the evil that he did. But how could he? Maria was dead.

Well, he decided he could do it by defending his victim, defending the good in his victim and becoming good himself. He told everyone how good she was and that he wanted to become good. He made a public announcement of his horrible crime and again asked God, the family, and the community to forgive him. Then he went to live with priests for the rest of his life working and praying, making up for what he had done.

He realized, Nathan, that his best friend turned out to be the person that he killed, because she cared about the life he would have after his death. That's a real friend. Your best friends, Nathan, are in heaven now, and their names are Brian and Aaron.

Nathan, if only you knew our Brian. Brian would have been your friend here on earth, too. Brian was your age, Nathan. He was only six months older than you. He was born only two hours away from here.

At the same time you were going to kindergarten, he was going to kindergarten. When you were learning how to read and write, ride a bike and play ball, Brian was learning the same things. He would have been your best friend.

When you had a hard time in your life, when your brother died, Brian was struggling with a sad situation, too. He knew how it felt to have a broken heart. He would have tried to cheer you up, Nathan, to help you through it. He wouldn't have let you fall like your so-called friends did.

Brian never saw the color of a person's skin, Nathan. He played football with Black and white players. He went to high school with Black, white, Asians, and Hispanics. He was friends with them all. They loved him, Nathan, and are so hurt over what you have done to him.

Brian volunteered at an inner-city school and hospital, and it didn't matter to him what the children looked like. You would have liked our Brian, Nathan, if only you had given him a chance.

He would have let you drive that Blazer, Nathan. He would have given you anything he had. Brian had such a big heart, Nathan. It hurt him to see others suffer, physically and emotionally. He wanted to stop people's suffering. That's why he wanted to be a doctor. He never wanted to hurt anyone. Isn't it so awful, Nathan, that you caused him so much pain? Brian must have been so, so sad and hurt on that hill knowing that one human being could be so cruel to another. Are you sorry for inflicting such pain? If only you knew him, Nathan. If only you had given him a chance. You didn't know Brian. Yet, you hated him. An innocent with no reason to be hated. You hated him and you hurt him. You terrorized him and Aaron on that hill. You made him feel your hate and you put such fear in his heart because your heart is cold.

Why hurt a stranger, Nathan, just because other people hurt

you in your life, and they did and I know that, but the pain you suffered should have made you want to alleviate pain, take pain away, not inflict it.

If you had love in your heart, Nathan, like Brian did, you never could have done this, and my deep sorrow is knowing that our Brian suffered for no reason. His brother Chris is suffering. The whole family suffers. His girlfriend is suffering, Nathan. Students from high school and college are suffering knowing there is such evil in the world, and you allowed it to work in you.

I know what a man is, Nathan. My son Brian was a man. My son Chris is a man. They were men long before they were eighteen years old. They grew up living honest lives. No one was ever afraid of them. No one ever thought of my sons as bullies. They were best friends to everyone around them.

You have a dangerous weapon, Nathan, and it's not a gun. It's fear, and you use it to make people obey you. I imagine there are many people who have seen you coming and they were afraid, children who maybe would run away, but no one was ever afraid of my Brian, not because he wasn't strong, because he was.

There is no one, Nathan, that is dead because of my Brian. He was a man. Brian would have been a real friend. He could have taught you how to be a man. Brian could have showed you that a real man is a protector, a provider of good things, a person who knows how strong he is and how much he can do to others, good and bad, and controls himself to do only the good.

My son Chris is here today. You just heard him. He's just like his brother. Many brothers would rise up and try to kill the person who killed his brother, but there is no violence in my Chris's heart. If he was given the chance to kill you, Nathan, he would not do it. The idea would never even come into his head. Chris is a real man. He's a good and honorable man. I know my sons, Nathan. The one in heaven and the one on earth are praying for you.

There are many men in this room, Nathan, but you are not

one of them yet. There were only two men on that hill that early morning of May 31, 1999, and you were not one of them. A real man doesn't need a gun, Nathan. A real man is powerful inside doing what is right, choosing good over evil. You and your friends that walked around with concealed guns are not men. You're babies, weaklings, fakes. You see, doing what is wrong, like you and Terrell and Brandon have done, that's easy. So you're babies. Doing what is right is hard, and that's what men do.

The two men on the hill are in heaven now, and they are your best friends. They want to greet you one day in heaven, but you have to want it, admit your horrible past, control yourself, and make up for what you've done.

Face yourself, Nathan. See what's inside, and then face God and do whatever he tells you. God is amazingly good, and he can change you, but he won't do it without your cooperation. When I look in your eyes, Nathan, I see anger. I don't see the peace that Jesus brings, but it can be there.

You're starting to learn, I suppose, what prison life is like, and probably the worst thing is losing your freedom, not being able to wear what you want to wear, eat what you want to eat, do what you want to do when you want to do it. You have no idea who to trust and not to trust. You have no one watching your back. You're on your own.

If you don't change, Nathan, the horrors of prison will stay with you forever, because if you don't change, Nathan, you will go to hell. There really is a heaven, and there really is a hell.

I want to tell you what heaven is like. In heaven you are fully alive and filled with happiness that will never end. In heaven you could never become sad again, never hurt, never angry, never jealous, never envious. None of the things that cause trouble on earth are even possible in heaven. In heaven you are constantly happy and constantly enjoying everything good and that happiness is always increasing.

In heaven there are no devils to tempt you. There is nothing unpleasant, nothing you have to avoid because everything in heaven is beautiful, beautiful, and it will never change. In heaven you are alive, perfect, and will never suffer. In heaven you will love everyone, and everyone will love you, and that's what you want, to be loved.

You will have perfect peace and your enjoyment will never end. You will feel God's love and all the saints' love. You will see them and be with them, and not one of them will hate you or be mean to you, ever.

But this is what hell is like. First, in hell you realize how good and wonderful God and heaven are and you know that you will never have it. That causes pain.

Next, you realize that hell will be forever. Do you realize I'm saying forever, Nathan? That means no end, ever. What could be the worst possible thing a person could do to be sent to hell? Kill somebody or watch somebody be killed.

In hell you are in constant pain, constant fear, and you are filled with hate, hate for yourself and hate for everyone else. There is no love in hell. In hell everyone hates everyone else. You are surrounded by hate like Brian and Aaron were when they were surrounded by you and Terrell.

In hell you will always want to be loved but never will be loved. In hell you will want some happiness but will never have it. You will want your pain to stop for just a short while, but it never will.

And there are physical sufferings in hell, too, Nathan. For instance, in hell you're extremely thirsty, and there's pain from that, but you will never have a drink. Knowing that you are going to suffer forever increases the pain forever and there's no escape.

In hell, Nathan, everyone smells like decaying flesh, a smell strong enough on this earth to make people physically sick, but there are billions of people that smell like that in hell.

In hell you will know it is your fault that you lost heaven. You will not be able to blame anyone else, and you will hate yourself forever. The things that you wanted on earth you will want even more in hell, but you will know you could never have them.

In hell you will see all that God has done for you while you were on this earth and how you spit in his face. In hell you will wish you could die to avoid the pain but you can't.

I don't want you to go to hell, Nathan.

Shame on those who say they care about you and haven't told you these things, Nathan. They want you to get away with murder. They want you to live another sixty or some years on this earth and then go to hell forever. Shame on them.

Shame on your lawyers who didn't tell you to plead guilty so that you could start on the path to heaven, because you are guilty and you have to say so.

Shame on all the witnesses that paraded up here yesterday to make excuses for you. That's not real love, Nathan. Real love cares about your life after death.

Nathan, you didn't show any kindness to Brian or Aaron, and you don't deserve any kindness now, but God is good and even now he's showing you mercy, which is undeserved kindness, and he will every day for the rest of your life.

But in prison you can die at any time, in any manner. If you die tonight, Nathan, you will go to hell. You have to do these things. You have to admit that you killed Brian and Aaron. You have to ask God to forgive you. Ask the families to forgive you. Ask the community to forgive you. You have to promise to do only good things from now on. You have to accept your punishment without any complaint. I believe you can do those things, Nathan.

Nathan, I loved my Brian so much. He's my son. He's with me right now. My heart is broken in a thousand pieces.

I said at Brian's funeral that my arms ache to hold him one

more time, and they still ache. I want my Brian back. Can you give him back to me, Nathan? You're the one that took him. Can you let me see him one more time? Can you let me say "Bri, I love you" one more time or say goodbye to him? I miss him, Nathan. He's my son. I need him. Can you turn back the hands of time like you said yesterday and give him back to me whole again? Can you keep yourself from putting that gun to my Brian's head? Can you see his pain on that hill and have pity on him? Could you listen to his plea for mercy and grant it? You can't do that now. Only God can give life, and only God should take it.

If only you hadn't done this, Nathan, I would have my Brian, and you would have your freedom, but losing your freedom in this life is not as bad as losing your soul forever.

Our lives are changed permanently. Now yours should be changed, too, but by that I mean you took a lot of good out of the world by taking Brian and Aaron. Now you have to put goodness back in.

After this life, Nathan, each one of us will go to heaven or hell. As long as you are on this earth, you can choose. Choose heaven, Nathan. I'm praying for you. God bless you, Nathan.

The following statements were made to Terrell Yarbrough on September 27, 2000, in Jefferson County, Ohio, court during the penalty phase of his homicide trial.

CHRIS MUHA TO TERRELL YARBROUGH

I heard someone earlier this week saying Terrell hadn't been given a fair trial; that he didn't have a jury of his peers. I heard the same thing expressed in the newspaper by someone from the local NAACP just before Nathan Herring's trial. The person who made that statement explained what she meant by it: Nathan's jury was all white. His peers, the only ones who could judge him fairly, were Blacks. Do we realize what is being said here?! Does this not promote the idea of "separate but equal" that Blacks fought so hard to abolish some forty years ago? If the only ones who can judge Terrell honestly are Black people, what does that say about the races? It says we are so different as to be unable to relate to each other. We are separate, but equal. Martin Luther King Jr. would shake his head in dismay if he were here witnessing members of his own race destroying what he fought so hard to abolish.

Does this mean that I understand what it's like to grow up as a Black person? That this jury understands what it's like to grow up Black? Of course not. But in order to be a Black person you must first be a human person. And that is why the civil rights movement fought so hard against the language and the idea of separate but equal. We are all human beings. At our most basic level, we are the same. I am your peer, Terrell, because I am a human being. I am in this whole thing we call life with you. What is most basic to all of us is that we have human life. And the wrongfulness of murder is something that applies to all human beings, whether that human is Black or white, male or female, pre-born or near death, growing up in a hard part of Pittsburgh or living at 165 McDowell for the summer. To say that Terrell can't have a fair trial because his jury is all white is to fail to realize that what has happened here is not about you being Black. It's about the fact that two human beings have been killed. That and that alone is why we are here.

But there is something else we are in together, Terrell, something even more important, and that is the whole process of salvation. That's right. We are in this together. Yet you wanted to separate that, just as that woman wanted to separate Blacks and whites. But you wanted to go even further. You weren't just separating your race from another race. You were separating yourself from all other people. And so you wrote on that piece of cardboard, "Only God Can Judge Me." And the eminent psychologist Dr. Brams told us that it was your attempt to make yourself look smart. And what a contrast this clear and complete statement was to the scribble of your notepad! But apparently, she didn't see the need to take that into account. Based on her expert opinion, it was your attempt to look smarter than you are. But as we both know, she was wrong. As we both know, "Only God Can Judge Me" is the title of a song by Tupac, a rapper from New York. Was he one of the rappers you told people you knew? Was he the inspiration for what you did? And who else is being influenced by Tupac's music?

Unfortunately, Tupac was more right about that than he knew. God would judge him, and a lot sooner than he had expected. And as you have said, God will judge you, too. And you are right: God alone will judge you after you die. But that, Terrell, is entirely different from the judgments passed on your actions here, today. For the Bible tells us that only God will judge us. But it also tells us to confront our brothers in their wrongdoing. And why should we do this? Because unless you change, you will not go to heaven. And, in that sense, Terrell, we are in this salvation thing together, too. And anyone who makes excuses for you is not helping you into heaven. Anyone who makes excuses for you does not ultimately care about your soul. Does your family here care about your soul? They have made lots of excuses for you: He doesn't have a jury of his peers; he wasn't raised well; he used to be a good boy until he met Nathan and Brandon. You — his family and friends — if you really love Terrell, why do you make excuses for him? Why do you not, instead, tell him to be truthful? You have all driven here to Steubenville each day for this trial, and that is commendable. But where were you when Terrell was growing up? Where were you when he came to Steubenville and met Nathan and Brandon? You have driven out here each day for this. Why did you not drive out here earlier when Terrell was first here? Why did you not drive out here and show him how much you love him and are concerned for him? If you are truly concerned for him, then you will be concerned about what matters most: his soul. If you are truly concerned about that, you will stop making excuses for him and you will show him that you love him by helping him to change.

And what about your lawyers? Do they care about you, Terrell, or are they making excuses for you, too? Do they want you to change? Or do you believe them when they tell you that you are too dumb to think normally? I don't believe that. We heard your own lawyers say that you are borderline retarded. Do you think that's true? I don't. And Mr. Olivito and Ms. Carinci, how dare you act as though the reason Terrell did this was because he is borderline retarded. How dare you act as though it is mental retardation that leads to such things! Mentally retarded people are the simplest, most honest, and most lovable people I know. Anyone who knows or has a mentally retarded child ought to be outraged at how you and your expert witness have insulted them.

And what about this expert witness, Terrell? What about Dr. Brams? Did she care about you? Or did she make excuses for you, too? As far as I could tell, all she did was embarrass you. And she, too, made excuses. She tells us that you didn't choose to commit these murders, but then, later, she says you were being compassionate when you showed the police where the bodies were. She said you could have chosen to do otherwise. So first she says you don't have free will, and then she says that you do. What is it, Terrell? Dr. Brams was not being straight with you, because she doesn't care about what matters most for you.

But there was one thing she said that spoke volumes about what is happening here.

She said that what you have known for your whole life is

people telling you one thing and then doing another; people telling you that they love you and then not showing it, not actually doing the hard action of loving you. And you know what? She was right. You say that you are responsible, but then your family says that you don't have a fair jury. What is that, if not an excuse? Mr. Olivito says that he is not making excuses for you, then proceeds to tell everyone that you are retarded. What is that, if not an excuse? Dr. Brams says she is not giving excuses, and then says that you didn't choose to do what you did. What is that, if not an excuse?

Terrell, all of these people have told you one thing and then done another, just as when you were growing up.

But there is at least one person who has said one thing and actually gone through with it. And she had done this because she loves you and is so concerned about you. This woman is not a member of your family, it is not your co-counsel, and it is not Dr. Brams. It is my mother. Even before you showed the police where the boys were, before she even knew you, she stood up in front of a packed church and chose to forgive you. And every day since then, she has fought back feelings of anger and rage. She has prayed for you every single day, so that you will change. That, Terrell, is love. That is a person who loves you.

And there are others here, too, who pray for you, despite the anger and rage they fight. And they are the ones who truly love you. And I, Terrell, have prayed for you every day since May 31. But do you know who the first person to pray for you was? It was Aaron. Immediately after you shot him. And do you know who the second person was? It was my brother, after you shot him. How ironic it is that the people to whom you showed such hatred were the first ones to pray for you. They love you now more than anyone. And they will never cease to pray for you. We heard Mr. Olivito say that he and the jury were more connected than you had ever been with anyone in your life. Well, he forgot about two people. Because Brian and Aaron are more connected to you, now, than you can even know.

And because of them, Terrell, I stand before you now, and I offer my forgiveness to you. I forgive you not because you had a rough childhood, because that is not an excuse. I forgive you not because you were depressed, because that is not an excuse. I forgive you because I have been forgiven. And I want so much to believe that you are truly sorry for what you have done. But until you willingly accept your punishment and change your life, I can't believe you.

What, then, about the death penalty? Does forgiving mean that I don't want the death penalty? Initially, the answer to this question was very clear: I don't want the death penalty. This is, in fact, what the Catholic Church teaches. You see, my Church is about life, both this life and the next. And her teaching on the death penalty is based on the sanctity of life. Thus, the death penalty is wrong, unless it is the only way to protect life. I had known all of this in the past year and didn't think that the situation of either Nathan or you, Terrell, was one in which the death penalty was necessary to protect the lives of others. But only recently have I heard what you have been doing since put in jail. I now know that you have helped someone try to hang himself and have gotten into at least three fights, the most recent in which someone's nose was broken. I was also made aware that you threatened the lives of everyone in prison who testified against you. And so I am left to wonder, "Is the death penalty necessary to protect the lives of other prisoners?"

What's more, is it in some way necessary to protect you, yourself? How long will someone like you last in a maximum-security prison with the worst of criminals? Would you last longer there, or while you sat on death row for at least ten to fifteen years? I have struggled a lot with this question the last few weeks and didn't make up my mind until just yesterday, when Dr.

Brams said that what you wanted most in jail was to be isolated. And nowhere but death row are you guaranteed to be in isolation. So that confirmed it for me. I did indeed want the death penalty, but I do not want you to die. There are those who might scoff at this, but it is precisely because I don't want you and the other prisoners to die that I am in favor of the death penalty. More precisely, I want you to be on death row, but I don't want you to die.

Do I want the same for Nathan Herring? No. He hasn't shown himself to have the same problems in jail as you have. Based on what we know (and that is all that we can go on), there is not the same threat to himself or to others. And so there is no need for the death penalty for him.

Some might see this whole thing as an elaborate attempt to justify the death penalty. Some might think we want it in Yarbrough's case because he was found to be the principal offender. Nothing could be further from the truth. Just because Nathan was not found to be the principal offender doesn't mean he was not, indeed, the principal offender. And the opposite is true for Terrell. But more importantly, it is absurd to think that someone who pulls the trigger is any worse than someone who just breaks into their house, just helps beat and kidnap them, just helps march them up a hill, and just watches without interference as they are both shot. No, the accomplice is just as bad as the principal offender and to think anything different is to miss the gravity of being a participant and an accomplice to such an act.

It is for no other reason than the protection of life that I do not want the death penalty for Nathan Herring. And it is for no other reason than the protection of life that I do want the death penalty for Terrell Yarbrough. You, Terrell, will be unable to threaten anyone, to beat up anyone, to kill anyone. And you, in turn, as best as I can judge, will have a longer life. You will also have the isolation you desire, an isolation which I hope will give you more motivation to change yourself and make up for what you have done. I will be praying for you every day. But more importantly, Brian and Aaron will be praying for you, too, as they have been since 5:30 a.m., May 31, 1999.

I can only hope that you find that same motivation wherever you end up.

RACHEL MUHA TO TERRELL YARBROUGH

I am Brian Muha's mother, and I can think of no better way to describe myself except to say I am Chris Muha's mother, also. I have two wonderful sons. I am that beautiful boy's mother, Terrell. You did not even know his name, Terrell, and did not care.

It is so hard, so painful, to look into the face of my son's killer … just to say those words is unbelievable. The son that I held when he was born, that I rocked, quieted, loved, protected — as much as I could — and watched and helped grow into a kind, compassionate, loving young man who would have been kind to you, Terrell, if you had let him. A mother never imagines she would have to face her son's killer; that she will have to stand in a courtroom and look at someone so young, so little — and so mean — and let the horrible truth sink in that this person — you, Terrell — took a gun in your hands and became the cold-blooded killer of my son. That you looked at Brian's face after having shot his dear friend, Aaron, and you saw his silent look of realization that "his time was up," as you so flippantly put it. That last look on his face of knowing, knowing that you were going to kill him, that you did not care if he died, that you did not think of him as a person who deserves to have his life — more than that, that you hated him and what he stood for. He knew that there was no use pleading for his life. You put that gun to his head and pulled the trigger anyway. My poor Brian. What a lonely, terrible way to die.

There were prayers going up to "Father God" last week in

the hallway by your family and friends, asking him to "set you free" — free from a guilty verdict. Those prayers, I am sorry to say, mock God — as if he would want a killer set free to kill some more. God is Truth and Justice, Terrell. The truth is, you hurt and killed two innocent boys. You did those things, Terrell, and you have to face yourself and see how bad that makes you. Then you pray to God, our Father, to set you free. Free from sin, Terrell, not from prison. Prison may be the only place that saves you. Justice demands that you be punished and others be protected from you. That is exactly what the dedicated police officers, prosecutors, judge, and jury have done. If I had to mention one person who did his job exceptionally well, I would say it was Detective Lelless, who was ridiculed in this courtroom by Mr. Olivito, your lawyer, Terrell.

You should be ashamed, Mr. Olivito, to have said those things. I could not have more respect for Detective Lelless, and I will always be grateful to the people in Steubenville, Father Scanlan, and everyone at the university, from the mayor and city manager on down who worked so hard to find Brian and Aaron, to find the vicious killers and to bring us to this conclusion today. I also want you to know, Mr. Olivito, how surprised I was when you said, "If only Brian Muha had waited one more day to come to Steubenville." Mr. Olivito, Brian and Aaron were exactly where they were supposed to be that early morning of May 31, 1999. They were not in the wrong place at the wrong time. Your client, Terrell Yarbrough, and his friends Nathan Herring and probably Brandon Young were in the wrong place doing the wrong things.

And so that you do not feel singled out, Mr. Olivito, I also want to say that for sixteen months now we have had to endure the humiliation caused by local gossips starting soon after Brian and Aaron died, such as local radio talk shows that allowed their hosts and listeners to spread false rumors about Brian, Aaron, Andrew Doran, and other students who lived in or visited 165

McDowell. They lied when they said there was a drug connection between the killers and Brian and Aaron. You know that no one owed anyone money, don't you, Terrell? They came up with the ridiculous lie that Andrew Doran was involved in gun trafficking, and they also had no right to criticize Andrew personally. If anyone has a question about Andrew Doran's character, they can ask me and I will tell them about the Andrew Doran I now know. These people didn't stop to think about the pain Brian's and Aaron's friends and family were already enduring and how these lies were like stabbing us in the heart.

I want you to know, Terrell, that when Brian looked at you that early morning, he saw the hate in your eyes, he saw the viciousness in your face, but I know he didn't see the color of your skin. He didn't care about skin color, as you and your so-called "friends" seem to. He didn't hate people because of their skin color — he didn't hate anyone. Hate is madness of the heart — it makes people mean — and Brian's heart was, and is even more so now, beautiful. There is a woman in Steubenville named Loretta Johnson, a Black woman who came to me after Brian and Aaron were found and told me about Brian helping her out at her home — she is very poor and her home needed repairs. Many of the Franciscan University students do the same.

You needed a real friend in your life, Terrell, and Brian and Aaron would have been that for you. A real friend, Terrell, cares about you so much that he or she tells you when you are wrong and when you are bad. A real friend helps you shape up and doesn't stop at anything to help you become a man. A real friend would tell you to take responsibility for what you have done, admit it publicly, be sorry for it, and welcome your punishment. I don't think anyone sitting there as family or friend has told you to do those things. They are not your friends, they don't care about your soul. They don't even care about their own souls, because they don't care about the truth. One of your relatives said you were convicted on "hearsay," but I don't think she knows what hearsay means or she wouldn't have said that on TV. Your poor mother, who thinks she is doing the right thing by saying you are a "good boy" and that she "supports" you doesn't realize that this is her greatest opportunity to be an honorable mother — for maybe the first time? — a real mother who doesn't waste her time, money, and energy on drugs while her children suffer, but a mother who will help you get to heaven because right now, you are headed for hell. You see, she called you "good," but how do you define a good person if not [by] their actions? And for your mother to say she supports you — well, *support* means to "hold up," to "advocate." In other words, to help someone in what they are already doing and thinking. Terrell, you need someone to undo your thinking and retrain you to do the right things.

Do you know what, Terrell? You and Nathan were not the only ones with weapons that night. Brian and Aaron had weapons, too. So did Andrew. Powerful weapons. More powerful than your weapon, Terrell. I have one. I would say that almost everyone on this side of the courtroom has one. You had one, too, for a short while. You didn't even know that what you had around your neck was more powerful than what you had in your hand. What you took from Brian — or did he let you have it? — was a rosary: a blessed object that helps us pray. It's more powerful because it leads us to heaven where everything is beautiful. Your gun will take you right to hell, where everything is disgusting. But you can have this weapon in prison, if you like. You see, when we pray the Rosary, we think about the life and death of the greatest Man that ever lived, Jesus Christ.

Brian and Aaron knew the power of the Rosary, and they knew that Mary, the Mother of Jesus, would watch over anyone who prayed it and would help them in the hour of their death. We are told to live our lives like Jesus and then we will go to heaven. So we think about what Jesus did while on earth as we pray and move our fingers along the beads. We spend a lot of time thinking about Jesus' death. You see, early one morning, while it was still dark and Jesus was praying in the garden, some men came. Cowardly men. Weak men who let evil enter into their hearts. And they took Our Lord and they beat him. They hit him in the face and spat on him. They whipped him and pushed thorns into his head and tried to humiliate him. And that was not enough to satisfy their hate. They took him to a hill and made him climb it. He fell three times trying to climb that hill, but they had no pity on him. Then, at the top of Calvary, they killed Jesus in a horrible way. And they watched him suffer. He was an innocent man — all he ever did was love. But his death brought us heaven.

Well, almost two thousand years later, and early one morning while it was still dark and while Brian and Aaron were asleep, some men came. You were one of them. Cowardly men. Weak men, filled with the same evil that filled the hearts of Jesus' killers. And you beat our sons. You hit them in the face and head. And seeing their pain was not enough to satisfy your hate. You took them to a hill and made them climb it. How many times did they fall, Terrell? Then you tried to make them do humiliating things while they were in such pain. Finally, on the top of Brian and Aaron's Calvary, you killed them in a horrible way. They were innocent boys, trying, trying, trying to live their lives the way God wanted them to. Now, they live in heaven, and they actually want you in heaven with them one day. They are praying for you, Terrell. They are your best friends. Talk to them. Ask them for help. They will tell you to be kind while in prison, to stop fighting and hurting and then maybe, one day, you will see them in heaven.

Of course, we don't know what happened to the cruel men who killed Jesus. Did they ask forgiveness and live better lives, or did they stay bad and end up in hell? You have the same choice they did: You can change and hope to go to heaven, where everything is perfect, or you can stay the same and go to hell. In hell, you will be in pain all the time, forever. You will be in fear, forever. You will hate yourself and hate everyone else — and they will all hate you.

Choose heaven, Terrell.

Terrell, you don't deserve any kindness — you didn't show Brian and Aaron any kindness. But Almighty God, who has the power and the right to take your life right now, is showing you mercy because you are his child, too. He is giving you time to change. But you never know how much time you will have. You could die tonight. Admit what you did and ask forgiveness. Then, start to make up for it, Terrell.

Terrell, our lives are changed forever — and yours should be, too. Our lives are emptier, sadder, lonelier. We can't have Brian and Aaron back, not in the way we were used to. Your life can be emptier, sadder, and lonelier than it has been, but it doesn't have to be. That's up to you. Turn to God, Terrell, and you can have a happy life, even in prison.

I will pray for you.

APPENDIX B

Rachel Muha's Talk at the 2021 Night of Champions

The following address was given by Rachel Muha at the Night of Champions on October 14, 2021.

Good evening everyone. Welcome to our Night of Champions. Don't you just love that title: Night of Champions? That means there are heroes, survivors, men and women, girls and boys fighting the good fight: running the race. We all love to be around champions.

But are there any champions living in the inner city?

Life in the inner city is hard. More often than not, it's miserable. I know two young men who grew up in miserable circumstances and grew so hateful that they didn't care about innocent people's lives. They killed. And they actually said, after they were caught, that they just wanted to know what it was like to kill someone. Can you imagine? And they said that quote, "After we killed the first one it was even better killing the second one." Do you notice they didn't even know the names of the boys they killed — and didn't care? These two young killers are named Terrell and Nathan, and they need your prayers. Who did they kill? They killed Aaron Land and Brian Muha, my son. Two young men who were sound asleep and expecting to get up the next morning and go to summer classes at Franciscan University. Two young men who when they closed their eyes to sleep that night didn't know they would be awakened by pain so unbelievable — pain from a vicious assault — that they couldn't see, couldn't move their broken jaws — could hardly walk. But were made to walk and climb — climb a hill to their deaths.

People asked then and still ask, "Why?" I didn't have that question because the answer to it is all around us: We live in a broken world. Instead, the question in my mind was, "What?" "What do we do now, Lord?" And the answer gave meaning to Brian's death and to the reason we are all here tonight. What do we do in the face of evil? We work with God to bring good out of it. We do what we can to bring justice out of an unjust act and we show mercy because God shows mercy to us. When I asked, "What do we do now?" the answer came back: "Love the children who are growing up just like Terrell and Nathan grew up." So I should go into a part of town where I don't know anyone or know anything about and start to help? The answer: Yes. And that's how the Brian Muha Foundation and Run the Race were born. And that's how we get to the question: Are there champions living in the inner city?

The following is from a *Columbus Dispatch* article. The men and women in these stories represent some of the moms and dads of our Run the Racers. Imagine being a child and seeing your mom or dad doing the things described in this story. Here it is:

> Nowhere in Columbus is there an area more plagued with prostitution and drug abuse than a 3-milespan [*sic*] of Sullivant Avenue that … covers parts of two neighborhoods: the Hilltop and Franklinton. …
>
> Mary Jo's Carryout at Sullivant and Hawkes [is] … a hub of activity 24/7. It's a regular post for the women of the streets, … drug dealers, and those buying anything they shouldn't. …
>
> The cars … pull up in front of the carryout for hours, like the line at a drive-through. …
>
> Across from the carryout, a woman named Linda sat on a curb slumped over and sweating … as the cars rolled by. The 37-year-old was too sick from drugs to worry about customers.
>
> She once had dreams of being a nurse, but the discovery of crack cocaine 13 years ago shattered all of her hope. She has worked on Sullivant since."*
>
> On Sullivant … the black car with tinted windows slowly circled the elementary school, lurking as the children climbed down the bus steps and headed for the first day of school.
>
> Joe Williams didn't take his eyes off the car as he stood guard over the playground that early August morning. …
>
> "That's a drug car," Williams, 58, said. "They are

*Bethany Bruner et al., "As City Prospers, West Side Corridor Remains Avenue for Drugs, Prostitution," *The Columbus Dispatch*, February 16, 2020, https://www.dispatch.com/story/news/crime/2019/10/20/as-city-prospers-west-side/1698618007/.

looking for customers."[*]

At an elementary school.

Sullivant Avenue is just two blocks from our Run the Race Center. Sixty-two percent of the residents on the Hilltop are white; 18 percent Black; 12 percent Hispanic; 7 percent other. It has the highest rate of fatal opioid-related overdoses in the city.

Last week a report was completed that said there are at least seventeen active gangs in the inner city of Columbus with more than 470 members. Those Columbus gangs do anything and everything necessary to keep their territory and their customers. Even things like dismemberment and burial in concrete. On the Hilltop. Where our Racers live. Houses they walk by every day. Stories they are fully aware of, unfortunately, because they hear the adults in their lives talking about it, worried about it or involved in it.

There are more than one thousand vacant houses in the three West Side precincts. There is a tremendous trash problem and the only ones benefiting from that are the rats. Yes, rats. In full view. In the alleys where children walk back and forth to school.

Columbus police officers were dispatched, in one year to fifteen thousand calls of fights, robberies, narcotics, shots fired, just in this one section of Columbus. And that is before counting murders. Precinct 19, which encompasses the Hilltop where the Center is, had more homicides than any precinct in the city.

People are starting to notice that the root of the problem is the breakdown of the family — people like the president of the NAACP in Columbus and the new police chief in Columbus, the first Black woman to lead the police department.

---

* Holly Zachariah, Jim Woods, and Mike Wagner, "Longtime Sullivant Avenue Residents Determined to Stay on the Street They Call Home," *The Columbus Dispatch*, February 23, 2020, https://www.dispatch.com/story/news/crime/2019/10/20/longtime-sullivant-avenue-residents-determined/1654451007/.

Chief Bryant said recently: "We have repeat offenders: fifteen-, sixteen-, seventeen-year-olds who are on their fifth and sixth gun crimes. What I have found is that when you go into some of these homes to meet the parents/guardians there is drug addiction, there is extreme poverty, there is illiteracy. We need to help heal the family." Police Chief Bryant also said that she is not at all in favor of defunding the police and in fact more resources are needed to train and maintain a good police force.

Two of our Racers wrote on Facebook recently — one is sixteen years old. Please excuse her grammar:

> All my life i ain't never really had a dad, my dad was locked up all the way until i turned 11 years old, he left me when i was 4 years old — for choosing bad things over me and my sister then after he got out he was always worried bout women. nobody knows the hurt i live with everyday; nobody knows the stuff he had put me thru nobody knows the pain that I've felt my entire life.

The other Racer, now nineteen years old, said, "life should be so much more than fighting, drugs & drama. so many lives have been took in the last 3 years. so much hurt. i hate to say that i hate the generation ive grew up in but theres no love no loyalty no peace makes me so sad."

There was a shootout at Holton Park recently. That's the rec center we used before we moved to where we are now. Twenty to thirty rounds, the neighbors said. The children in the neighborhood were under beds or crouched in corners — crying and screaming.

Ideally, a child should grow up in a home, school, and neighborhood that nurtures, encourages, sets good examples, and provides positive experiences that create strong, healthy pathways in their brains. Trauma imprints itself in the whole body, mind, and spirit. Trauma radically alters the way children, and the adults that children become, are able to live their lives.

Now what do we do? It sounds like there are no champions living in the inner city. And this problem is too big. Let's give up.

No, let's not. You are not doing that — the proof is that you are here tonight. And I am not doing that. No.

We do have champions who help us help the children. There is always trepidation when one starts to name names because the last thing I want to do is leave anyone out, so please know that we are grateful to all of you — our board, our very hard working and wonderful Night of Champions committee — haven't they done a wonderful job! — our sponsors, our donors — everyone. Thank you!

A Champion's work comes in many different forms.

Bishop Brennan is one of our champions. He came to The Run the Race Farm and had a meal with our ten homeschooled Racers. He talked to them like a friend and a father. He told them about growing up in New York. He told them about a game he used to play, taught them how to play it and they play it often. He blessed them. Now Bishop Brennan is going back to New York, and we will miss him.

Two other champions are Kathleen and Wade Wiant. Kathleen and Wade's son Collin died during a terrible hazing event at Ohio University. Kathleen and Wade successfully got a law passed in Ohio, Collin's Law, that not only makes hazing a felony in Ohio but also a crime if you become aware of hazing and don't report it. Kathleen and Wade are champions.

Then there is a good friend of ours, Lisa Burgess. Lisa's son Corday was murdered outside his home. Corday left little children who miss their father very much. Lisa is heartbroken but not defeated. Lisa started a nonprofit in Corday's memory with the desire to help children who have lost a parent to violence. Lisa is a champion.

There are the Friends of the Foundation who raise money for and supply pajamas, coats, food and more to our Racers every year. There is J. J. Solinger and Terence Dials from OSU, who gave our Racers a really fun basketball clinic a few months ago. There is St. Francis de Sales High School and their Run the Race Support Club that has been wonderful to our Racers. There is Mary Kay Fenlon, who is here tonight, and she is running for judge in Franklin County Municipal Court. There is Tammy Adler Foeller and Leslie Kristoff who started OpenDoor Columbus, an outreach to women recuperating from drug addiction.

There are the wonderful McEnerys who own MAC Construction and always come to our aid when something has to be replaced or repaired at the Center or the Farm. And there is Bryan Hamilton and Shawn Golden of Hamilton Contractors who are helping us with a big project we will tell you about a little later.

Of course there are the amazing Christ Child Society women and also Janet Jenkins' Food Crew who provide breakfast, lunch and early dinner to our Racers every day. That's a lot of food — and a lot of love. They are champions.

There are the many volunteers who help tutor at our Day School — one of the hardest but so rewarding volunteer opportunities we have. There is Penny Barrick and Hannah Mohler who teach our Racers about horses with firsthand experience with Penny's horses — every Friday. There are the five young men, high school seniors from Columbus Academy and Olentangy High Schools who started their own non-profit a month after COVID invaded. They help young people through tutoring and hands-on experiences. They help the Racers a lot. Their nonprofit is Columbus Equal Opportunities Association, and I hope you have the chance to meet them tonight. They are Sidd, Sammy, Dakshin, Min-Song, and Aryaman.

There are other volunteers who are behind the scenes: like a friend who supplies copy paper and ink; another one who is collecting Halloween costumes and making treat bags; another one who has a Thanksgiving food drive for our families every year; other compassionate people who buy new washers and dryers, donate money for a used car for a young mom, or who collect donated furniture for our Racer families. We have an army of champions!

Of course, my champion is Brian. He loved children and wanted to serve them. Just like Kathleen and Wade, Lisa, and so many others, we miss our children. I read this quote by Dietrich Bonhoeffer. He said:

> There is nothing that can replace the absence of someone dear to us, and one should not even attempt to do so. One must simply hold out and endure it. At first that sounds very hard, but at the same time it is also a great comfort. God does not fill the emptiness but much more leaves it precisely unfilled and thus helps us preserve — even in pain — the authentic relationship.

Just recently I read a beautiful poem. I don't know who wrote it. It goes like this:

> **You Don't Just Lose Someone Once** *
> You lose them over and over,
> sometimes in the same day,
> When the loss, momentarily forgotten,
> creeps up,
> and attacks you from behind.
> Fresh waves of grief as the realisation hits home,
> they are gone.

---

*Donna Ashworth, "You Don't Just Lose Someone Once," September 16, 2021, https://donnaashworth.com/2021/09/16/you-dont-just-lose-someone-once/.

Again.
You don't just lose someone once,
you lose them every time you open your eyes to a new dawn,
and as you awaken,
so does your memory,
so does the jolting bolt of lightning that rips into your heart,
they are gone.
Again.
Losing someone is a journey,
not a one-off.
There is no end to the loss,
there is only a learned skill on how to stay afloat,
when it washes over.
Be kind to those who are sailing this stormy sea,
they have a journey ahead of them,
and a daily shock to the system each time they realise,
they are gone,
Again.
You don't just lose someone once,
you lose them every day,
for a lifetime.

It's true. And it hurts. But we will gain them back again one day. One day when we are reunited. That is the hope, made possible by the Divine Mercy of Jesus Christ. That is what we are so grateful for — grateful to our God who loves us all so much that he wants us together forever.

At the Center, we live by these truths: Every human being shares an origin — they come from God; they share a nature — made in the image and likeness of God; and a destiny — to be united with God. Any differences are secondary, and actually can enrich us all. We as humans can, and should, build each other up as members of the same family. God's family.

I mentioned our Day School. We are homeschooling eighteen young Racers and we have at least that many volunteers who come in every week to tutor them one-on-one. Not one child came to us at grade level. Most are two to three years behind. But they are eager to learn, they are smart, they are delightful. Still, they come to school with heavy burdens on their minds.

There are the two boys whose cousin was killed recently, stabbed twenty-two times. The boys are haunted by that memory. These boys lived in foster homes for six and a half years of their lives. They are only eight and twelve years old.

There is another little eight-year-old whose father died one month ago of COVID pneumonia. There is another twelve-year-old who told us about the bullet that came flying through their house and almost hit his sister. There is the sweet Racer whose mother is on drugs and our Racer has been in five foster homes in her eleven years of life.

There is the twelve-year-old who has to take out the trash every night and is afraid. He sees needles and other Skid Row–type trash strewn all over the ground.

There is the brother and sister who live with their grandmother because their mother and father are drug addicts. An uncle also lives with them and when he is drunk — which is often — things are not good. The children live in fear of him and in fear of being taken away.

There are the three sisters whose mother won't let them near the windows because there is a *trap house* — where drugs are sold — behind them, and there are fights and shootings. There are the Racers who aren't allowed to play in their backyards because of the homeless camping out in the alley.

These are all real-life stories of only eighteen Racers whom we are homeschooling. But all of our Racers, three hundred to four hundred of them, have the same stories.

The parents/grandparents of our Day School students are happy to have their children with us. One said simply: "My boys love coming to your school."

Another said, "Thank goodness for all the amazing people who work with the kids. We are so blessed to have such giving, sweet, smart people who are a part of the Foundation. I thank God for you all."

And a third, from a very young mom who is raising her children and her sister's daughter. She wrote:

> You [and she means all of us who are active at the Day School] are doing something soooo so so amazing and for my kids to be apart of that is worth everything. I can only imagine how much you've put into this, and for that im forever grateful. Tbh I think about this school that you've created a lot. Like more than you'd ever imagine, to see that there's still people like you is beyond words. And I want to do more. I would like to be something in your school. Whether that be a once a week volunteer or help with projects or whatever it may be I want to be there! Anything you may need plz lmk.

Do you notice she says "I would like to BE something in your school." I love that. She wants to BE — she doesn't just want to do. She wants to BE. That is our goal for all of our Racers.

But back to the original question: Are there champions living in the inner city?

I'm often asked, "Are you making a difference? How many lives have you changed?"

I feel sad for people who ask that question because they don't realize the value of just one human life. The worth and dignity of just one life. One life makes it all worthwhile. What if our little Mason, for example, was the only child at the Day School? Should we say, "Well, he's only one boy. What difference does he make?" Why help a little boy whose mother died of an overdose, whose father is a cocaine addict, who comes to us dirty and hungry and mischievous? Should we say we won't teach him to read and write and do math? Should we say, "We won't feed him." Of course not! Would our other compassionate supporters say, "We won't clothe him." No! You see, one person's life is worth giving everything for. It can transform that life and transform the people who are opening their hearts to him. The people who give without counting the cost. It can't get more beautiful than that. That's priceless.

There are always new children coming into the Center. And so we start all over, almost every day, teaching, helping, loving.

At the Center and Day School we spend so much time reminding children that they don't have to resign themselves to the excuses that seem to be in the air in the inner city. It's true, life hasn't been fair. But what will they do about it today? We tell them that whatever they wake up to each morning: a stolen bike, empty stomachs, parents who aren't there physically or emotionally, don't let it stop them from running their race. That they can experience more in life if they will get over the excuses and get on with living. They can have excuses or they can have results — but they can't have both. And then we tell them what we know is the most powerful, most encouraging, most exciting message of all. We tell them: "You can do all things in Christ who strengthens you!"

Having heard all that, you can understand why I say the children of Run the Race are incredible champions. Imagine what they live with — and live without. Many of you have seven- or eight-year-olds in your families, or twelve- thirteen, or fourteen-year-olds. Picture them. Our Racers, just like your children, do things kids do: Maybe they sleep in or they don't sleep enough;

they struggle with their school subjects, they argue with their siblings. They get moody. You've seen it. You know how that affects the children and you. Now add hearing gunshots every night, seeing fights every day, seeing drug deals and overdoses, knowing your parents are in prison or dead. Imagine how that affects the children.

But given a chance and given confidence in their worth, their compassion comes out. One Racer saw a homeless man across from the Center one day and couldn't rest until she took him a sandwich — her sandwich. One Racer who spent her whole childhood wondering why her mother would leave her is the first Racer to play with the little ones and give them some happiness. During COVID, groups of middle school/high school–age boys would come to the Center doors when they saw our cars in the parking lot and plead: "When are you going to open up again? When you do, will we have field trips? Will we have food? Can we stay now for a little while?" They don't want to be on the streets.

There is Martine. He started coming to Run the Race when he was twelve. He is twenty-three now, married, and the father of three. He works full time at a very hard job pouring concrete every day. The only one in his family with a high school diploma, full-time job, married with children. He coaches little league football. He comes and visits us and brings his children. He tells us how much he learned at Run the Race. Then there is a Run the Race girl also in her twenties now and a longtime Racer. She wrote to me recently and told me she remembers asking me why I didn't have the radio on in the car when I was taking her home, and I told her because she was more important, and I would rather talk to her. She said that made all the difference to her. She felt loved. You never know. Then there is the grown-up Racer who said she learned responsibility and how to be a "real adult" by watching all of us at the Center.

And there is a champion who is only eighteen years old. She has been coming to the Center on and off since she was twelve. I say on and off because she is the oldest of ten, and there is no dad, or dads, around. Mom is in and out of the house, gone for days, back again, out again. There was a grandmother around to help but she is not there anymore. An observant neighbor noticed and told us of the needs of the children. They are afraid to get separated into various foster homes. The eighteen-year-old is working at Little Caesar's making next to nothing and trying to keep her siblings together. She is a champion.

Love reigns in the inner city. And YES, there are champions living in the inner city.

I have seen it over and over again: the human spirit, fortified with the grace of God, overcoming evil and bringing good into the world. That's what our Racers do. That's what Run the Race is about.

So friends, come and see. See the joy on the children's faces. See the relief on their faces as they walk into the Center and away from the streets. See their childhoods return. See what a difference your help is making. See the champions you are helping create.

Thank you for being champions to our champions. God bless you.

Works Cited

"2 Missing University Students in Steubenville Believed Dead." *Plain Dealer* (Cleveland, OH), June 4, 1999, p. 17-A.

Bailey, Brittany. "Vandalism of Columbus Non-Profit Streamed Live on Facebook." WNBS 10 CBS. April 22, 2020. https://www.10tv.com/article/news/local/vandalism-columbus-non-profit-streamed-live-facebook-2020-apr/530-356e7833-8583-4d69-a3db-a46f19b3fe51.

Brian Muha Foundation. The Brian Muha Foundation/The Run the Race Club. www. https://www.brianmuhafoundation.org/.

Catechism of the Catholic Church, 2nd ed. Washington, DC: Libreria Editrice Vaticana–United States Conference of Catholic Bishops, 1997/2019.

Crompton, Janice. "Prosecutor Wants 2 Back on Death Row." *Pittsburgh Post-Gazette*, February 9, 2006, p. B-1.

———. "Retrial Begins in '99 Slayings of 2 College Students."

Pittsburgh Post-Gazette, October 18, 2009.

———. "Revisiting Painful Past." *Pittsburgh Post-Gazette*, October 18, 2009, p. A-13.

"Death Penalty." Office of the Ohio Public Defender. opd.ohio.gov/law-library/death-penalty.

"Death Penalty" Gallup. news.gallup.com/poll/1606/death-penalty.aspx.

"Death Penalty Sought in Murder of 2 Ohio Students." *Columbus (OH) Dispatch*, December 13, 2006, www.pressreader.com/usa/the-columbus-dispatch/20061213/page/41.

Eiler, Sean. "Steubenville Officials Get Eye-Opening View of the Realities on the Hilltop." WTOV9 Fox (Steubenville, OH), October 18, 2016, wtov9.com/news/local/steubenville-officials-get-eye-opening-view-of-the-realities-on-the-hilltop.

Emeigh, John Grant. "Plans Finalized for KKK Day Events." *Herald-Star* (Steubenville, OH), July 8, 1999, p. 1.

"Franklinton, Columbus, OH Crime." AreaVibes, www.areavibes.com/columbus-oh/franklinton/crime/.

Gillespie, Charley. "Mom Buys House to Reclaim It for God." *Plain Dealer*, July 23, 2000, p. 5-B.

Gilligan, David. "Mother Forgives Son's Killers." Associated Press, June 10, 1999.

Hanauer, Amy, Emma Schubert, and Zane Steiber. "Race in the Heartland: Ohio in Focus." Policy Matters Ohio, October 10, 2019, www.policymattersohio.org/research-policy/fair-economy/work-wages/race-in-the-heartland-ohio-in-focus.

Huff, Christopher. "Forensic Psychologist Says Yarbrough 'Mentally Deficient.'" *Intelligencer* (Wheeling, WV), September 27, 2000, p. 1.

———. "Herring: I Always Wanted Bigger and Better Things." *Intelligencer*, August 30, 2000, p. 9.

———. "Herring's Fate Nears." *Intelligencer*, August 30, 2000, p. 1.

Huff, Christopher. "Pathologist Testifies in 'Boo' Herring Case." *Intelligencer*, August 23, 2000, p. 11.

"Issue of Jurisdiction Arises in Slaying of 2 Collegians." *Philadelphia Inquirer*, June 9, 1999, p. B2.

Lafferty, Mike. "Details of Slayings Make Defendant Cry." *Columbus Dispatch*, September 19, 2000.

———. "FBI Forensic Experts Link Defendant to Slain Student's Truck." *Columbus Dispatch*, August 25, 2000.

———. "Jurors See Crime Shots as Trial Opens in Slaying of Franciscan University Students." *Columbus Dispatch*, August 22, 2000, www.dispatch.com/news/newsfea00/aug00/393254.html.

———. "Woman Helps Searchers Look for Missing Son." *Columbus Dispatch*, June 4, 1999, p. 1A.

Lagatta, Eric, and Marc Kovac. "Report Claims 17 Gangs with about 480 Members behind Nearly Half of Columbus 2020 Homicides." *Columbus Dispatch*, October 6, 2021, www.dispatch.com/story/news/2021/10/06/report-many-columbus-homicides-involve-gang-group-members/6009299001/.

Lash, Cindi, and Ann Rodgers-Melnick. "Students' Bodies Found in Robinson." *Pittsburgh Post-Gazette*, June 5, 1999, p. 1.

Lash, Cindi, Johnna Pro, and Diane Juravich. "Following the Trail." *Pittsburgh Post-Gazette*, June 4, 1999, p. A-14.

Lash, Cindi. "3 Say Suspect Admitted Killing 2 College Students." *Pittsburgh Post-Gazette*. August 25, 2000, p. B-3, https://old.post-gazette.com/regionstate/20000825steubenville5.asp.

———. "Convicted Killer Apologizes as Steubenville Jury Weighs Sentence." *Pittsburgh Post-Gazette*, August 30, 2000, p. 1, https://old.post-gazette.com/regionstate/20000830steubenville6.asp.

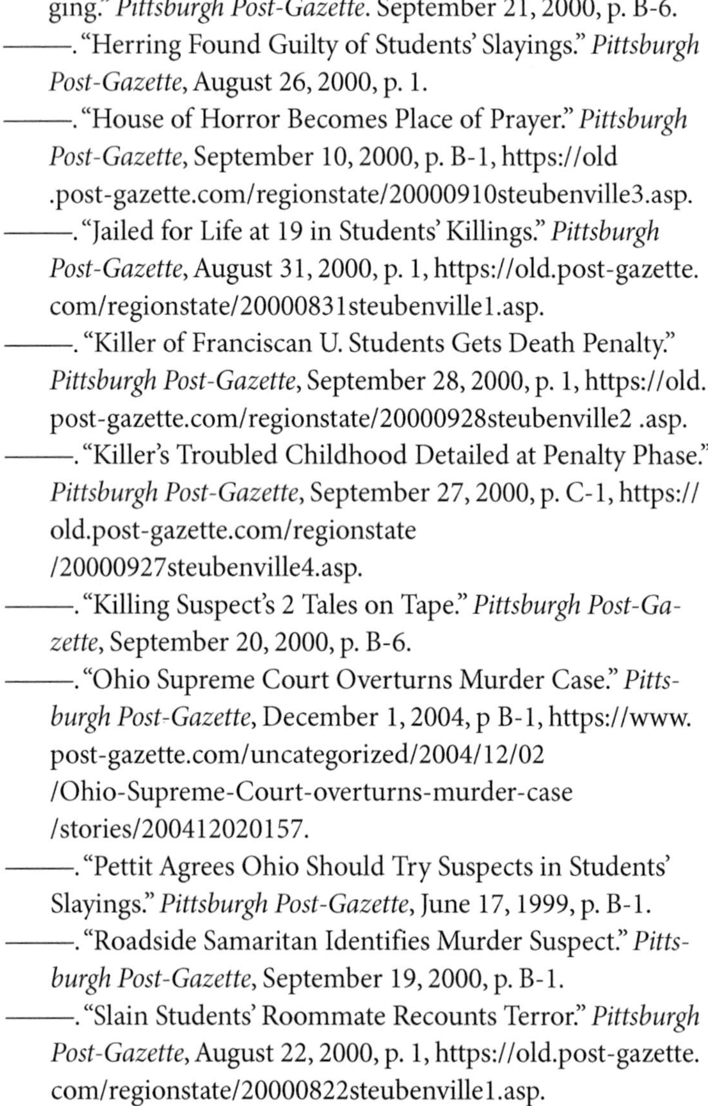

———. "Defense Attacks Accounts of Suspected Killer's Bragging." *Pittsburgh Post-Gazette*. September 21, 2000, p. B-6.

———. "Herring Found Guilty of Students' Slayings." *Pittsburgh Post-Gazette*, August 26, 2000, p. 1.

———. "House of Horror Becomes Place of Prayer." *Pittsburgh Post-Gazette*, September 10, 2000, p. B-1, https://old.post-gazette.com/regionstate/20000910steubenville3.asp.

———. "Jailed for Life at 19 in Students' Killings." *Pittsburgh Post-Gazette*, August 31, 2000, p. 1, https://old.post-gazette.com/regionstate/20000831steubenville1.asp.

———. "Killer of Franciscan U. Students Gets Death Penalty." *Pittsburgh Post-Gazette*, September 28, 2000, p. 1, https://old.post-gazette.com/regionstate/20000928steubenville2 .asp.

———. "Killer's Troubled Childhood Detailed at Penalty Phase." *Pittsburgh Post-Gazette*, September 27, 2000, p. C-1, https://old.post-gazette.com/regionstate/20000927steubenville4.asp.

———. "Killing Suspect's 2 Tales on Tape." *Pittsburgh Post-Gazette*, September 20, 2000, p. B-6.

———. "Ohio Supreme Court Overturns Murder Case." *Pittsburgh Post-Gazette*, December 1, 2004, p B-1, https://www.post-gazette.com/uncategorized/2004/12/02/Ohio-Supreme-Court-overturns-murder-case/stories/200412020157.

———. "Pettit Agrees Ohio Should Try Suspects in Students' Slayings." *Pittsburgh Post-Gazette*, June 17, 1999, p. B-1.

———. "Roadside Samaritan Identifies Murder Suspect." *Pittsburgh Post-Gazette*, September 19, 2000, p. B-1.

———. "Slain Students' Roommate Recounts Terror." *Pittsburgh Post-Gazette*, August 22, 2000, p. 1, https://old.post-gazette.com/regionstate/20000822steubenville1.asp.

———. "Steubenville Jury Continues Deliberations." *Pittsburgh Post-Gazette*, September 22, 2000, p. C-5.

———. "Trial Told Fatal Bullet Matches Those Found in Suspect's Home." *Pittsburgh Post-Gazette*. August 24, 2000, p. B-2. http://old.post-gazette.com/regionstate/20000824steubenville6.asp.

———. "Yarbrough Found Guilty." *Pittsburgh Post-Gazette*, September 23, 2000, p. 1.

Law, Mark. "Bullets Match in Student Murder Trial." *Herald-Star* (Stuebenville, OH), August 24, 2000, p. 1.

———. "Guilty Plea in 1999 Killings." *Intelligencer*, July 9, 2010, p. 1.

———. "Prosecutor Says Urge to Brag Was Yarbrough's Undoing." *Herald-Star*, September 19, 2000.

———. "Witness Sees Accused Driving BMW Stolen from Pittsburgh Woman." *Herald-Star*, August 22, 2000.

Medick, ErinMarie. "Family, Friends Put Brian to Rest." *Columbus Dispatch*, June 10, 1999.

Milicia, Joe. "First of 2 Suspects on Trial in College Students' Slaying." *Plain Dealer*, Tuesday, August 22, 2000, p. 7-B.

Morgan, Kate. "How a Mother Turned Her Grief into Goodness." *Woman's Day*, December 8, 2019, www.womansday.com/life/inspirational-stories/a29833029/brian-muha-foundation-info-rachel-muha/.

Muha, Rachel. "I Don't Want My Son's Killers Put to Death." *Catholic Times* (Columbus, OH), November 28, 1999, p. 16.

Norman, Tony. "Mother Shows Color of Bravery in Forgiveness." *Pittsburgh Post-Gazette*, September 1, 2000, p. E-1. https://old.post-gazette.com/columnists/20000901tony.asp.

"Ohio Law Expands Homicide Prosecution." *Pittsburgh Post-Gazette*, April 13, 2005, p. B-4.

Ostendorf, Kristen. "Franciscan University Conducts Memorial Honoring Slain Students." *Pittsburgh Post-Gazette*, September 3, 1999, p. E-1.

Pope Francis. *Fratelli Tutti*, par. 241–243, vatican.va.

Pro, Johnna A., and Ann Rodgers-Melnick. "Abducted Pair Feared Dead." *Pittsburgh Post-Gazette*, June 3, 1999, p. 1.

"Prosecutor Wants Trial to Be in Ohio in Killing of Two Steubenville Students." *Plain Dealer*, June 7, 1999.

"Prosecutors Say Murder Suspect Bragged about Killings." NBC4 (Columbus, OH), September 18, 2000.

"QuickFacts: Columbus City, Ohio." United States Census Bureau, www.census.gov/quickfacts/fact/table/columbuscityohio.

Raghavan, Sudarsan, and Barbara Boyer. "Students' Slayings: Worlds Clash." *Philadelphia Inquirer*, June 6, 1999, p. 1.

Rishell, Grace, and Robert Dvorchak. "Our Hearts Go with You." *Pittsburgh Post-Gazette*, June 7, 1999, p. A-13, https://old.post-gazette.com/regionstate/19990607steuben3.asp.

"Robed Klansmen Rally, Rant in Steubenville." *Plain Dealer*, July 11, 1999.

Rodgers-Melnick, Ann. "Insight: Prodigal Sons Celebrate a Life." *Pittsburgh Post-Gazette*, June 6, 1999.

Schackner, Bill. "Ohio Grand Jury Could Hear Homicide Case in July." *Pittsburgh Post-Gazette*, June 6, 1999, p. A-22.

"Slain Students Are Found." *Philadelphia Daily News*, June 5, 1999, p. 6.

St. John Chrysostom. "St. John Chrysostom's Letter to St. Maron." The Maronite Foundation, https://maronitefoundation.org/MaroniteFoundation/en/MaronitesHistory/67

State v. Yarbrough. 104 Ohio St. 3d 1. 2004-Ohio-6087, web.archive.org/web/20070101042353/http:/www.sconet.state.oh.us/rod/newpdf/0/2004/2004-ohio-6087.pdf.

The Catholic Foundation. https://catholic-foundation.org/about/.

"The Mission of Franciscan University of Steubenville." Franciscan University of Steubenville, www.franciscan.edu/mission-charisms/.

"Transcript: Victim's Impact Statements in the Nathan Herring Case." *Pittsburgh Post-Gazette*, September 27, 2000. old.post-gazette.com/regionstate/20000831impacttrans9.asp.

Troiano, Laura. "Her Son's Murderers Sentenced, a Mother Reflects." *Catholic Times*, October 22, 2000, p. 1.

"Victim Brian Muha's Mother and Brother Address Yarbrough in the Courtroom." *Pittsburgh Post-Gazette*, September 28, 2000, http://old.post-gazette.com/regionstate/20000927muhastatements9.asp.

About the Author

Gretchen R. Crowe is editor-in-chief of OSV News, the national and international Catholic wire service reporting on Catholic issues and issues that affect Catholics. As editorial director of periodicals at OSV, she also oversees the content of many print and digital publications, including *Our Sunday Visitor*, the only national Catholic weekly newspaper in the United States; OSV's two clergy magazines, *The Priest* and *The Deacon*; its children's magazine, *OSV Kids*; and online content on SimplyCatholic.com, TeachingCatholicKids.com, and RadiantMagazine.com. An award-winning writer and photographer, Crowe is the author of two other books: *Why the Rosary, Why Now?* (OSV, 2017) and *Praying the Rosary with St. John Paul II* (OSV, 2019). Crowe lives in Fort Wayne, Indiana, with her husband and three children.